Listen! First Time Landlord Me!!!

Martha Jarvis

Disclaimer

All Rights Reserved. Any unauthorized reprint or use of this material is strictly prohibited. No part of this book may be reproduced or transmitted in any form or by any means, electronic or mechanical, including photocopying, recording, or by any information storage and retrieval system without express written permission from the author.

The information provided in this book is for informational purposes only and is not intended to be a source of advice or credit analysis concerning the material presented. The information and documents contained in this book do not constitute legal or financial advice. They should never be used without consulting a financial professional to determine what may be best for your needs.

The publisher and the author do not make any guarantee or other promise as to any results that may be obtained from using the content of this book.

You should never make any investment decision without consulting your financial advisor and conducting your research and due diligence. To the maximum extent permitted by law, the publisher and the author disclaim any liability if any information, commentary, analysis, opinions, advice, and recommendations in this book prove inaccurate, incomplete, unreliable, or result in any investment or other losses. Content contained or made available through this book is not intended to constitute legal or investment advice, and no attorney-client relationship is formed. The publisher and author provide this book and its contents on an "as is" basis. Your use of the information in this book is at your own risk.

Dedication

To my cherished parents, whose untimely death profoundly impacted my life.

To my two sons, whose memories always motivate me, and one who passed away too soon.

To my sister, whom I will always treasure for her love and presence.

I will always be indebted to my spouse, son, brothers, sister, and grandchildren, whose love and support have strengthened me.

Of course, I also want to thank all my readers for coming on this adventure with me. This book is for you!

Acknowledgment

I want to start by thanking God for His direction, grace, and constant support during this journey. All of this would not have been possible without His blessings.

I would especially like to thank Robert, whose support and faith in me motivated me to write this book. Your belief in my story has consistently inspired me.

Asher, Noor, and the whole staff have my sincere gratitude for supporting me during the entire process. Your commitment, knowledge, and support were crucial in making this project a reality. I appreciate your steadfast assistance and your presence.

To everyone who has been a part of this journey, your love and support mean the world to me.

About the Author

Hi there, everybody! Martha S. Jarvis is my name. I attended Anderson High School and was born in Anderson, Indiana. I enrolled in a personal awareness course at Anderson College after high school, where I graduated in the early 1970s with a certificate. Later, I spent almost a year and a half studying at Ivy Tech College, which helped to mold my perseverance and work ethic.

I've worked at several different professions throughout my life, and each one has taught me important lessons about perseverance and hard effort. My hobbies outside of work include singing and running, which make me happy and help me stay grounded.

I am a devout woman who incorporates her faith into all aspects of her life. I try to be a good example of leadership by prioritizing other people and trying to improve my community. I have established myself as a successful businesswoman and landlord because I am a diligent and astute entrepreneur. I handle each of these worlds with poise, tenacity, and a dedication to quality.

People around me are inspired by my commitment to honesty and faith, and I firmly think that everything is achievable with perseverance, hard effort, and a service-oriented attitude. I am honored to serve as a living example of what is possible when we uphold our moral principles and welcome the difficulties that life presents.

Preface

Becoming a first-time landlord was far more than just managing properties; it was about creating spaces where people live, thrive, and dream. When I began my journey as a landlord, I quickly realized that this role requires more than a basic understanding of real estate. It demands a commitment to building meaningful relationships, ensuring the safety of those who live in my properties, and striving to make a positive impact on their lives. This book is a reflection of the lessons, challenges, and insights I've gained over the years. It covers the practical aspects of property management—everything from tenant screening (which I learned the hard way) to maintenance, as well as the invaluable human side of being a landlord: empathy, resilience, and integrity.

I believe that by viewing property ownership through a lens of service, landlords can build successful businesses while also contributing to the betterment of their communities. Whether you're an aspiring landlord or a seasoned professional, I hope this book serves as a guide and an inspiration. It is meant to remind us all of the deeper purpose behind our work. May this book equip you with the tools, mindset, and perspective to navigate the challenges and embrace the rewards of this unique and fulfilling profession. Thank you for joining me on this journey.

With gratitude,

-Martha S. Jarvis

Contents

Disclaimer i
Dedication iii
Acknowledgment iv
About the Author v
Preface vi
Chapter 1: Struggling for Respect 1
Chapter 2: A Family Proposition 9
Chapter 3: Starting Small, Dreaming Big 11
Chapter 4: Seizing Opportunities 16
Chapter 5: Embracing Change 18
Chapter 6: Navigating Property Pitfalls 24
Chapter 7: Financial Realities 30
Chapter 8: Learning Through Action 39
Chapter 9: Setting Boundaries and Expectations 46
Chapter 10: Empowering Others, Empowering Myself 53
Chapter 11: Dealing with Deception 59
Chapter 12: Navigating Personal and Professional Challenges . 65
Chapter 13: The Toll of Tenant Troubles 73
Chapter 14: Taking Back Control 81
Chapter 15: Reflections on a Landlord's Journey 93

Chapter 1: Struggling for Respect

This chapter is a tribute to all current landlords and a roadmap for all future ones. As a landlord, I know the challenges of managing tenants, so I mean to "salute" them.

Consider yourself as the owner of a property, or possibly a portfolio of properties, motivated by a genuine desire to impact your neighborhood positively. Your ethos revolves around affordability, with cheaper rents and flexible deposit alternatives, all to assist individuals in finding a place they can truly call home. But ready for a voyage that will try your patience, strain your limits, and reveal the complexity of human nature in ways you never imagined.

I, too, began this path with lofty goals of lower rents and smaller deposits, motivated by a genuine desire to aid individuals in need. However, as time passed and the layers of human behavior were revealed, I came to a startling understanding. My kindness, it appeared, was frequently misinterpreted as naivety, a flaw to be used to the utmost degree by those with less noble intentions.

The truth is that the world of property management is a complex landscape in which idealism must frequently face hard realities. It is a domain where good intentions might be misinterpreted, and acts of goodwill can be received with suspicion or, worse, exploitation. Nevertheless, great lessons about fortitude, discernment, and the importance of finding a delicate balance between assertiveness and empathy can be learned from these challenges.

"We can't pay the deposit, but we'll make sure to pay the rent on time."

Sounds familiar?

Don't be misled by their promises.

It's a classic statement that all too frequently leads to disappointment. Trust me, I've heard everything. However, the harsh truth is that actions speak louder than words regarding property management. I discovered the hard way that generosity is frequently mistaken for weakness. Tenants are incredibly adept at spotting weakness and will take advantage of it if you show the slightest hint of weakness. Although it's a tough lesson to accept, every landlord needs to know it.

I have a simple, no-nonsense policy that states that you will not receive the keys if you cannot pay the deposit. Although it might sound severe, maintaining this border is crucial. I mean, this is a business, not a charity that I'm running. And in the business world, allowing feelings to cloud your judgment is unacceptable.

Thus, I offer advice to all the landlords: *hold onto your principles tightly.*

Don't let the sweet words of tenants sway you from your path. Remember, you're here for business, and sometimes that means making tough decisions. But in the end, it's worth it to protect your investments and maintain your sanity in the often chaotic world of property management.

Being a landlord requires a careful blend of compassion and commercial acumen. I want to help others, but I also have expenses to pay and property to maintain. And when tenants start pushing the boundaries, it's time to put on your landlord gear and lay down the law.

Take rent payments as an example.

You'd think it would be a simple monthly transaction, right?

Wrong.

I've had tenants who avoided my calls, ignored messages, and made more excuses than you could shake a stick at when paying rent on time. There was one occasion when it felt like I was pulling teeth.

Then there are the household rules. I'm not talking about anything dramatic here—just simple things like keeping the noise down and respecting your neighbors. But you'd be surprised at how many tenants believe these regulations don't apply to them.

I've dealt with everything from unauthorized pets to late-night parties that would make Animal House appear mild. It is enough to make you want to rip your hair out. Being a landlord can sometimes feel like tiptoeing through a maze of half-truths and fabrications. Whether intentionally or not, tenants often elaborate tales to evade their responsibilities or gain some advantage. When they are well past their due date, tenants offer myriad creative excuses for their late rent payments. From a mysteriously lost check in the mail to an unexpected expense that conveniently vanished into thin air, the stories can range from the mundane to the absurd. I remember laughing at their face because a five-year-old could have come up with better excuses than they said. People are not good liars- this is what 35 years of being a landlord taught me.

If pets are off-limits in the rental, a tenant might try to sneak them or lie about their existence to avoid any fees or consequences. This happened to me once, and I almost lost my cool.

Sometimes, tenants will go to great lengths to expedite maintenance requests or escape their lease early. From exaggerating or inventing maintenance issues to concocting personal crises like sudden illnesses or family emergencies, the stories can be as elaborate as they are implausible.

Imagine the shock of facing a tenant brandishing a gun when all you're asking for is the rent. Such was my reality when a payment dispute escalated into a terrifying confrontation. And all I did was ask for the payment I deserved.

There was a time when I found myself standing outside a tenant's door, trying to reach them regarding overdue rent. Despite multiple calls going unanswered, I persisted, only to discover they were deliberately ignoring my calls. It took a call from a different number for them to finally pick up, feigning ignorance when confronted about their evasion tactics.

The key is to stay informed, keep an open line of communication with your tenants, and be clear from the beginning. Having a well-defined lease agreement, setting realistic expectations, and keeping detailed records will help you navigate potential bumps and address issues that arise fairly and effectively.

To prevent any potential falsehoods regarding damages, it's a good practice to photograph the property before and after it's rented out. These images are tangible evidence of the property's condition and any changes during the tenancy. If any discrepancies arise, you have visual documentation to refer to, ensuring clarity and accountability.

By being vigilant and proactive in seeking evidence, landlords can effectively address any potential dishonesty or breaches of the lease agreement, ultimately maintaining a fair and respectful rental environment for all parties involved.

Building a positive landlord-tenant relationship is a shared responsibility. One major aspect that sticks out is the importance of clear communication. I've discovered that open, legitimate, and straightforward communication with my tenants provided the foundation for mutual understanding and determination. Effective communication fosters a sense of belief and honesty when addressing concerns or clarifying desires, ultimately strengthening the landlord-tenant relationship. Another critical component is property maintenance. Respect for tenants entails maintaining a commitment to property upkeep. Responding to maintenance requests and ensuring vital services are operational meets legal duties and demonstrates a genuine concern for tenants' well-being and comfort. For example, when a tenant reported a leaky faucet, responding quickly alleviated their stress and demonstrated that I care about their living conditions.

Respecting the privacy and limits of tenants is also essential. Providing appropriate warning before entering rental apartments respects tenants' privacy and autonomy in their living environments. This technique instills residents' sense of security and trust, contributing to a positive landlord-tenant interaction. For example, providing tenants advance notice before completing routine inspections or repairs respects their privacy and fosters a pleasant relationship.

Rent payments on time are another sign of respect in the landlord-tenant relationship. Tenants display reliability and integrity by paying their rent on time and in full, contributing to the relationship's stability. In contrast, late or delayed payments can strain both parties' trust and communication.

Adhering to property rules outlined in the lease agreement is essential for maintaining order and harmony. Whether regarding noise, pet policies, or other guidelines, upholding these rules fosters a respectful and cooperative living environment. For instance, enforcing property rules consistently reinforces expectations and promotes mutual respect among tenants when addressing noise complaints.

Equity and fairness are also crucial. As a landlord, I am committed to treating all tenants with impartiality and respect, irrespective of their backgrounds or circumstances. This fairness builds trust and fosters a positive landlord-tenant relationship. Similarly, I expect tenants to reciprocate this fairness by honoring their obligations outlined in the lease agreement.

Conflict resolution is inevitable in any relationship, but how you address conflicts with tenants can significantly impact the outcome. By approaching disagreements with empathy, understanding, and a willingness to find mutually acceptable solutions, landlords and tenants can preserve the integrity of their relationship. For instance, engaging in open dialogue and compromise helped resolve the issue amicably when addressing a dispute over property maintenance responsibilities.

Adherence to applicable laws and regulations is non-negotiable. From housing codes to eviction procedures, landlords and tenants must uphold their legal obligations to ensure a safe and lawful living environment. This commitment to legal compliance fosters trust and accountability between both parties.

In diverse communities, cultural awareness and sensitivity play a crucial role. Acknowledging and respecting cultural differences mitigates misunderstandings and cultivates an inclusive environment that celebrates diversity. For instance, being mindful of cultural practices when scheduling maintenance activities demonstrates respect for tenants' backgrounds and traditions.

Maintaining a professional demeanor in all interactions is essential. From prompt responses to inquiries to fulfilling obligations promptly, professionalism contributes to a positive and respectful landlord-tenant relationship. For example, promptly addressing tenant inquiries or concerns demonstrates a commitment to customer service and fosters trust and goodwill.

Overall, the dynamics of respect in landlord-tenant relationships are intricate and multifaceted, encompassing clear communication, property maintenance, privacy, fairness, legal compliance, cultural sensitivity, and professionalism. Landowners and tenants can cultivate a harmonious and mutually beneficial living environment by prioritizing respect in all interactions.

Despite its challenges, being a landlord was a valuable learning experience. It equipped me with the skills to navigate diverse personalities and undoubtedly shaped who I am today. It formed a significant chapter in my life's story. Later in this book, I will delve deeper into the experiences that led me to this point.

Chapter 2: A Family Proposition

Life throws you curveballs, some faster than others. This one hit me like a rogue fastball right in the gut. My mom, bless her soul, had passed, leaving a void no amount of sorrow could fill. Then, bam, another blow landed on my doorstep – my brother. Don't get me wrong, I love the guy, but timing is everything, and he couldn't have been worse.

Here I was, freshly laid off. The taste of unemployment was clinging to my tongue like cheap whiskey. Every penny I'd earned from my last job, the money sent back home, had been chased down the dusty alleys of addiction. Yeah, I was a mess, drowning my sorrows in a bottle so deep I couldn't see the bottom.

So, there he stood, my brother, with this proposition about our mom's house on the old street.

"Want to buy it?" he asked bluntly.

Some might see that as a lifeline, a chance to snag a piece of the American dream. But it was just another complication, another burden to shoulder on my already wobbly legs.

The truth is, I never planned on becoming a landlord. The closest I came to real estate was the dingy apartments I'd bounced between, with peeling paint and that ever-present scent of despair. But there it was, the house, a constant reminder of a life well-lived and a future I wasn't sure I was equipped to handle.

The initial steps were a blur. Paperwork piled up like a snowdrift, legalese swirling around my head like a bad dream. There were lawyers, inspectors, and a circus I never knew existed. Everyone spoke a different language of mortgages and deeds, leaving me tongue-tied and frustrated.

It was a crazy gamble.

Here I was, a recovering alcoholic with a shaky past, diving headfirst into the world of property ownership. The odds were stacked against me higher than a skyscraper. But something clicked in that foggy brain of mine. Maybe it was the desperation, the need to prove myself, or maybe it was a deep-seated desire to honor my mom's memory. Whatever it was, it lit a fire underneath me.

This landlord business wasn't sunshine and rainbows. It was a constant battle, a war fought on multiple fronts. There were nights I questioned my sanity and moments when the weight of responsibility threatened to crush me. But like a stubborn weed pushing through concrete, a determination grew within me.

I learned the ropes, navigated the murky waters of real estate, and became the best landlord this city had ever seen.

Chapter 3: Starting Small, Dreaming Big

The initial period of being a landlord wasn't as smooth as I wished. Let me be honest: it was not easy because of my issues. It was amazing how quickly and effectively I got myself up to speed with the landlord business. My mom was no longer in this world; her house was on the street where I lived.

After her death, I was left alone. Growing up as the youngest child, I didn't get much attention. My sister and brothers were busy working at General Motors. However, their tough love philosophy taught me valuable lessons. Their philosophy was, *'If you're broke, that's your business,'* but in times of crisis, they would jump to come to my aid. I'm glad for the way they raised me; they made me who I am today.

To escape all these emotions, I started to consume alcohol, which did not come without its impact on my life. I was terminated from My job after I lost my mother. I went broke. I had spent all of my money on alcohol.

I had to struggle a lot; it was indeed a tumultuous time when there was no one for me, and I had to manage everything all alone, without any support or any monetary assistance. It was tough. However, these days have marked one of the biggest changes of my life. I wasn't aware that I would transform this much. The house my mother had was given away to my brother. That house was the only asset that was a link to my mother. It was one thing that cherished our memories together.

Nevertheless, once I came back from the suffering, I was even stronger. At that time, choosing to buy that house from my brother was one of the most important moments of my life. It was when I understood it was finally time to settle in some place. My brother owned the house. It took me no time to decide to put the money forward and give it to him. I had to save a huge sum of money to buy it.

I felt like this was what I was supposed to do, and from then on, I was budding towards a watershed. I started feeling down, checking real estate listings from one site to another, hoping I could find some investment experience. The enthusiasm for this new interest was so powerful that it seemed to burn inside me, so to say, taking me around the property ownership thing with a lot of vigor and enthusiasm.

I can still remember this particular day when I had a hectic mix of harsh suffering and joy due to the completion of business. By all means and for all reasons, I was firmly convinced that this just had to be the right thing for me to do. The deal was done, and I found I was the sole owner of the house I shared with my mother.

Nevertheless, the way of rendering was far from just a walk under beautiful trees. While settling in, several unexpected problems faced me with the mission to resist. From tenations over good repairs to liquidity problems, each impediment seemed to cast a shadow on the matter of me having finally owned the apartment.

***

Afterward, when I embarked on my journey as a landlord, I faced many setbacks. However, I kept trying despite being hindered from moving, and I couldn't quit; I persevered to succeed. Each hardship I have been through during my journey to becoming a landlord taught me an irreplaceable skill regarding the complexity of real estate operations.

There was no way that you could think ahead and anticipate any problem, as they were always coming unannounced. Unforeseen repair costs and financial strains sometimes cause these. Through them, I learned to be resilient despite the circumstances and never to give up.

From this, I gained deeper insights into properties and the roles one needs to play when owning a property. From my experience, I learned how sensitive budgeting should be, the painstaking importance of performing regular repairs, and the need for long-term planning to ensure the building operation goes smoothly.

Besides, I became a problem-solver, which involved finding the proverbial stick to eliminate a thousand obstacles I faced. My resourcefulness and adaptability have also improved. Each new challenge became a chance for self-improvement, and I achieved higher resoluteness, facing the new unexpected difficulties without fear.

The saying *"We are not shaped by but build our experiences"* is the only way to summarize my growth.

In retrospect, I appreciate the remarkable things I gained and progressed in my personality over these experiences. Through the bumpy road, I have come to be someone who understands life, knows more about people, and is not afraid to receive disappointments. When I land on my feet with every hurdle, I shall find myself stronger and ready to manage whatever ups and downs might await me as a landlord.

As a landlord, the hurdles I have encountered so far have considerably changed my strategy in property management and how I make decisions in the future. The wisdom I acquired from adversity remains timely and still shapes me to lead others toward their goals.

First of all, the abovementioned obstacles have developed true resilience in me. When I discovered resilience, I could live with the fact that I was meeting barriers, and every barrier was an opportunity to improve. With this strength as my rock, I have applied it to challenging times with great dignity and perseverance.

Additionally, these beginnings have brought me a wealth of knowledge that keeps shaping my decision-making. Today, I learned to see each new venture with a tall order of impartiality and caution. I carefully weighed the pros and cons before throwing in my lot for any commitment. I effectively evaluate and analyze properties before investing.

Those hardships have helped me understand life better as they have cultivated empathy and humbleness within me.

To summarize, the struggles that I faced during my first years as a landlord have been, undoubtedly, the ones that affect the way I deal with my property management decisions and everything that I am going to do next. They have awarded me additional characteristics- due to resilience and great responsibility.

Chapter 4: Seizing Opportunities

The turning point arrived unexpectedly, a twist of fate disguised as a leaky faucet. It wasn't exactly a eureka moment; it was more of a slow, dawning realization that gold, or at least sweat equity, was hidden in the neglected houses scattered around the city.

It all started with a call from a tenant in one of my recently acquired properties. The faucet in the kitchen was on the fritz, spraying more water on the counter than in the sink. Fixing a leaky faucet wasn't exactly brain surgery, but it felt like a monumental chore between work and the never-ending list of landlord responsibilities. So, I decided to roll up my sleeves and tackle it myself.

A strange sense of satisfaction washed over me as I wrestled with the rusty pipes under the sink. Sure, it wasn't glamorous work, but there was a certain accomplishment in fixing something myself. And hey, I saved myself the cost of a plumber. But more importantly, it sparked a curiosity about the inner workings of a house.

'What lurked behind the walls? How did the electrical system snake its way from room to room?'

It was like a puzzle waiting to be solved.

This newfound fascination didn't stop at plumbing. Driving around the city afterward, my eyes started to see things differently. The boarded-up bungalow on the corner wasn't longer an eyesore but a potential diamond in the rough. The peeling paint on a two-story house screamed "opportunity" instead of neglect. Everywhere I looked, I saw fixer-upper houses whispering promises of hidden potential.

The idea was exhilarating. Instead of waiting for tenants to call about leaky faucets, I could be proactive. I could find undervalued properties, roll up my sleeves, and breathe new life into them. The profit potential was undeniable, but the real motivator was the challenge: the chance to transform a neglected house into a beautiful, functional home for someone else.

Sure, there were uncertainties.

'What if I overestimated my renovation skills and ended up over my head? What if the housing market took a downturn right as I finished a project?'

Doubt gnawed at the edges of my excitement, but a surge of inspiration quickly overpowered it. This was a new chapter, a chance to build something from the ground up, literally and figuratively.

And so, with a toolbox in hand and a head full of dreams, I embarked on a new strategy. I devoured books on renovation, subscribed to every DIY channel I could find, and spent hours poring over real estate listings. The thrill of the hunt became addictive. Every fixer-upper was a puzzle waiting to be solved, a chance to make a profit and leave my mark on the city. The journey wouldn't be easy, but with a newfound determination and a healthy dose of optimism, I was ready to seize the opportunities ahead.

Chapter 5: Embracing Change

I never pictured myself wound up at the crossroads of the real estate investment business. This wasn't one of those decisions I had planned or thought of choosing as my career. But destiny, surprisingly, had a vision of its own — it got started with the loss of my mother, an incident I hadn't expected at all.

Losing her made me feel like I was hit by a freight train; I sank into an abyss of sorrow and bewilderment. It was tough to swallow the truth – that she was gone. I felt like the whole world had been removed from under my feet.

Yet, as time passed and the initial shock began to fade, I faced a choice: to remain with the sting of the past or welcome the new part of my life. I decided to follow the latter because every challenge hid some seeds of personal growth and change.

Hence, propelled by my eagerness, I faced the uncharted waters of property management. It was a real grind punctuated with many hurdles and setbacks, and from dealing with tenants to supervising repairs, every single day brought its specific problems. However, I realized that those problems helped me to become more efficient and determined.

At times, I debated whether I was the right person for this journey and moments when the weight of responsibility felt like it would fall onto me. At times, I used to think about whether I chose to enter into this. However, in times of darkness, I kept believing that struggle always paves the way to greatness.

When we think that nothing is left, that is often because we are so focused on the good taken away from us that we don't realize this is happening to give us room for something better. There was something greater waiting for me, which life was getting me ready for.

Of course, now, when I reflect on everything that had happened to me throughout this process, I can see that every adventure and hardship was nothing more than a stepping stone to get me to where I am today. Seeking to handle the unforeseen curves and bumps of my new profession did not mean just to put my skills to the test, but it was a pilgrimage of my inner self.

Through the unpredictability of life, I learned that embracing uncertainty is the best solution. Amid all this chaos, I learned to build a resilient, optimistic, and adaptable mindset and the value of having a positive outlook when facing challenges. It is expected to feel overwhelmed by the forbidding tasks and uncertainty when overcoming problems.

However, each failure became my chance, a chance for me to grow and move forward. I reframed obstacles as opportunities that helped me climb to the next level instead of stumbling blocks that discouraged me. This mindset shift empowered me to keep trying harder.

Resilience became my most cherished possession. Some days, the burden of all I was going through weighed so heavy that my whole spirit would break. On other days, failure was so inevitable that nothing I could do could help to prevent it. However, instead of giving in to desolation, I gained the strength to fight harder. I could not let my failure bring me down; instead, I used my strength to overcome the barrier even when my resolve and determination were already on the verge of quitting.

I established that adaptability was one of the pillars of my mentality. It was a career of which no one can be certain. It would have been catastrophic if anyone had even imagined the life plan. But I ceased to think as if there were a concrete path to the destination; I became more flexible at life changes and knew my way around new situations. I could switch tack, drawn on my inner reserves, to negotiate the unanticipated crises.

Yet, amidst the chaos, one lesson stood above all: the power of believing in oneself. It is sometimes difficult to believe in oneself when facing doubt; we tend to think we are not good or experienced enough. I resisted letting self-doubt become my prison. Instead, I built my strengths, making them the cornerstones of my unyielding self-confidence. I was challenged to accept that growth comes only after one walks past fear, and I tried to tread the path head-on and not in a cautious manner. Looking back on my journey, I'm grateful for the challenges I faced and the lessons I learned. Each trial and tribulation that catalyzed my growth propelled me closer to my goals. As I continue to navigate the unpredictable terrain of my career, I do so with a newfound sense of purpose and resilience. For I know that no matter what obstacles lie ahead, I have the strength and fortitude to overcome them

In life, there are times when the twists and turns seem like insurmountable obstacles, but I have learned to perceive them as a gateway to new experiences and personal development. My experience vividly demonstrates this fact; as I have gone through these difficulties, I have experienced the benefits of change. Sometimes, it is better not to be swift.

You have to learn the art of letting go. Although it is hard to understand, once you master it, you realize how much benefit and peace it brings you - there is power in letting things go. And this is going to open many new doors for you. Let Him decide your path when you give yourself in God's hands.

People can feel lost and frustrated when unplanned events occur. My struggles have taught me to regard these events as references to discovering unexpected routes and doorways to new opportunities. The path of life could be replete with unforeseen events - a job layoff, a broken relationship, or a health crisis. The key, however, is whether we are willing to grab the opportunity presented by each twist to grow or to sit and cry over what is lost.

Perhaps the most valuable lesson that I've learned is the importance of adapting. Confronting the unexpected is usually stressful, so you might feel subdued or drained.

However, we can always pull in our strength and stand out against the harshest challenges. These moments are the turning points when we discover how strong we can be.

Another aspect of embracing change is flexibility. Rigidity commonly leads to irritability when things do not go according to plan. However, by being flexible and adaptive, we can smoothly transition when situations change, and instead of observing it as a failure, we readjust our path and learn from it.

There are so many more important things to dedicate my precious life to than years of being inadequate or staying in a position that does not help my growth anymore. We can enter a reality of satisfaction and purposefulness that has never occurred before.

I can inspire people to be receptive to acceptance and follow suit by drawing on my own experience of accepting what cannot be altered. They have revealed that sometimes, when the road seems like the end of the world, there is still a way out for those who are determined to keep going.

Life is an incredible journey that never ends and leads us to get through the unknown curves of life.

Yet, it is also a journey that shows us different aspects of ourselves and makes us grow. Those roadblocks happen to be the building blocks to making our history.

I have learned the art of letting go the hard way, but we can improve our lives if we know it before encountering unforeseen events.

Therefore, I urge everyone experiencing unforeseen difficulties or feeling disoriented by change to embrace the experience. Have faith in your ability to bounce back and keep an open mind to new opportunities because that's when we frequently discover the best chances for our development and contentment.

Thus, even if my path into real estate investing was unanticipated, it has been one of personal development and revelation. Through this path, I've learned to put my faith in fate's unseen hand, knowing that it has much bigger plans for me than I could have imagined. I will always be appreciative of that.

Chapter 6: Navigating Property Pitfalls

It's easy to become engrossed in the thrill of discovering the ideal house or investment opportunity while buying real estate. But it's important to remember that hidden problems could cost you a lot of money and effort. As a helpful assistant, I strongly emphasize seeing any issues before purchasing.

A home purchase is a big financial commitment, so you must choose wisely. It's normal to concentrate on a property's advantages, including its size, price, and location, but it's also crucial to consider any potential problems that might take time to think.

Hidden damage is one of the biggest problems that can occur with properties.

Several things, such as structural issues, bug infestations, and water leaks, can bring on this damage. These problems can be challenging to find because a routine check might not pick them up. If neglected, though, they may require expensive repairs or potentially jeopardize the stability and safety of the building.

I've encountered these situations on more than one occasion when buying properties. One of the most unforgettable encounters was with a seemingly immaculate property. However, after a careful examination, I found a severe termite infestation on the property. The harm was done despite the previous owners' best efforts to conceal the problem. The property's structure had sustained significant damage due to the termite infestation, costing thousands of dollars in repairs.

Termites can be difficult to find and can do severe structural damage to a house. They can lurk in the ceilings, floors, and walls, and the damage may already be done by the time you notice the symptoms of an infestation. A termite infestation may be indicated by mud tubes, mushy or hollow-sounding timber, and abandoned wings outside the building. To prevent further problems, it's critical to take prompt action if you observe any of these symptoms.

These concerns range from little wall fractures to severe foundation issues. In certain instances, it can be challenging to identify these problems because a routine check might not reveal them. However, if ignored, they may result in serious safety risks and jeopardize the structure of the building.

A seemingly perfect property had one of the most significant structural problems ever. After a careful examination, I determined the property had severe foundation issues. The significant repairs took several months to complete, and in some instances, the extent of the repairs significantly diminished the property's value.

Various problems, such as faulty construction, soil movement, and water damage, can lead to structural concerns. Uneven floors, wall cracks, and poorly closing doors are a few indicators of structural issues. To prevent future problems, it's critical to take prompt action if you observe any of these symptoms in the future. When buying a property, it's crucial to be proactive to prevent these problems. This entails a comprehensive property examination, encompassing a termite assessment and a structural appraisal. A qualified inspector can see any possible issues and offer a thorough report outlining their findings. You can use this report as a reference while deciding whether or not to buy the property.

Awareness of any warning indicators of concealed damage is also critical. These indicators include water stains, foundation or wall cracks, and termite or rodent infestations. Prompt action prevents further problems if you observe any of these symptoms.

Occasionally, concealed harm could not become noticeable until after the acquired property. Any problems you find after the purchase need to be fixed right away. This could entail settling on a price for the repairs with the seller or employing a specialist to fix the damage.

In conclusion, finding any possible problems with a home is critical before deciding to buy.

By being proactive and performing a comprehensive examination, you can ensure the property is solid and safe and save expensive repairs. This approach is crucial, as I have personally experienced with termite infestations and structural issues. We request that you take the necessary safety measures to protect your investment and yourself.

The importance of thoroughly inspecting a property cannot be overstated. As a helpful assistant, I saw firsthand the terrible consequences of omitting this crucial stage in home-buying. When buying real estate, getting caught up in the excitement of finding the perfect home or investment opportunity is easy. It's critical to remember that unresolved issues may cost you much money and time.

Due diligence is the extensive inspection, confirmation, and research process before entering a real estate deal. It involves thoroughly investigating the property, its records, and all the pertinent information that might affect the deal's outcome.

Due diligence serves as a buffer against unforeseen problems and shocks for purchasers. It provides more insight into the state, worth, and related legal issues of the property and protects the deposit of your earnest money. Due diligence also benefits sellers by enabling them to market their property as favorably as feasible. By conducting thorough due diligence, they may resolve any possible problems or inconsistencies up front, increasing the property's appeal to a potential buyer.

Real estate brokers are essential in assisting their clients with due diligence. Their knowledge guarantees that all due diligence is completed effectively and per the law. Due diligence is the cornerstone of wise decision-making for investors. Conducting financial due diligence ensures that the investment aligns with your goals and expectations.

The due diligence stage is essential in any real estate purchase. Typically, it begins with signing the purchase agreement, and the seller accepts the buyer's offer. Legal due diligence involves examining the property's legal facets, such as the title, zoning laws, and any liens that may be in place. It also includes exploring the property's financial statement, property tax records, rental income history (if relevant), and any upcoming or projected expenses.

A property survey is frequently carried out to establish a property's borders and ensure that the land measurements correspond with the legal specifications. Getting title insurance is a typical step to safeguard the buyer's rights and ensure no unreported title concerns.

Exercising due diligence has several advantages. It guarantees that sellers show their property in the best possible light, helps purchasers avoid expensive surprises, and gives real estate brokers the knowledge and skills they need to support their customers.

Due diligence is necessary for investors to make wise investment selections.

Finally, buying a home requires careful consideration. Adopting a proactive stance and comprehensively examining the property is imperative, encompassing a termite assessment and a structural appraisal. By doing this, you can make an educated investment decision, prevent expensive repairs, and guarantee the property is stable and safe. Please take the required precautions to safeguard your investment and yourself as a helpful assistance.

Property appraisal is a crucial component of financial due diligence. Consider hiring the services of many appraisers to determine the property's market worth accurately.

These experts will assess the property according to its size, condition, and location, giving you a more thorough idea of its value.

Income and expense analysis is yet another essential part of financial due diligence. Reviewing past income and expense statements, investors can learn more about the property's economic performance and spot opportunities for cost reductions or rent hikes.

Additionally, running expenditures such as property taxes, insurance premiums, maintenance charges, and energy bills should be fully factored into the financial analysis. Setting aside money for management costs is crucial if the investor needs to oversee the property personally.

Chapter 7: Financial Realities

One of the biggest challenges I found as a real estate investor was securing funding for my projects. However, even though I had a solid business plan and could spot opportunities with a marvelous team, I could not actualize my vision without the money. This is when I approached the national bank.

I began by researching different ways of acquiring loans from national banks, their rates of interest, and terms and conditions before settling on one type of loan that would help me get money to buy and renovate houses and give me flexible repayment terms.

After doing away with other options, I chose a national bank that works closely with real estate investors. In readiness for this meeting, I set aside time to meet with the loan officer. I also prepared a package containing my business plan, financial statements, and an in-depth investment strategy analysis.

The loan officer saw how much work had gone into planning and asked me several questions to understand better what kind of business they were dealing with. Being open about where we want to be at various risk levels or even our financial position played a role in establishing trust between them and me.

Having perused my submission, the loan officer gave me a few choices: a commercial property loan and a line of credit.

I chose the commercial property loan with competitive interest rates and a ten-year repayment term. The loan officer explained collateral requirements, fees, and late payment penalties, including terms and conditions. I thoroughly reviewed all documents and sought clarification to comprehend what was expected from me in that agreement.

For you as a purchaser or rather an investor who is looking for financing through a national bank, here are some points that may help:

- Research different kinds of loans.

- Come up with a well-rounded package containing your business plan and financial statements.

- Be open about your intentions, potential risks, and financial condition.

- Create rapport with loan officers and keep open lines of communication.

- Study carefully the terms and conditions of loans before signing any contract.

You can secure funding that will enable you to move your business to another level by adhering to these tips while being persistent.

The Challenges of Securing Financing: My Personal Experience

Although I perceived my debut loan as a real estate investor with many expectations regarding my income flows, not the interest rates, I was shattered by the high charges charged by the national banks when I started shopping for loan options. Every other loan came with exorbitant charges, and its interest would take away most of my profits.

But it seemed like every bank had similar rates, so I couldn't tell which one to borrow money from. In this dilemma, I had to choose between securing a costly business loan and putting my company's financial soundness at stake or just waiting until I had more capital to put into it. In conclusion, a modestly higher interest rate on the credit was worth taking since it would give me the funds required to expand my enterprise.

Another hurdle was unfamiliar economic expressions. I was a real estate investor who dealt with the prices of properties, rental returns, and remodeling costs. Nonetheless, when I started applying for loans, I was confused by financial jargon. What does "amortization schedule," "collateral," or "covenants" mean?

I spent hours reading through financial documents to understand them. I asked my loan officer for each word in simple English, but it was still insufficient to tell me exactly what I was getting myself into. It made me feel so bad, overwhelmed and scared that the wrong move could ruin me.

Despite my attempts to ensure that everything went well during the process of loaning, there were still issues that came up unexpectedly. This included last-minute additional paperwork requirements from the bank that delayed loan approval. Besides, a complex web of regulations and compliance matters increased my stress.

Reflecting on these challenges, I see that they were just part of the standard loan process. All borrowers have similar hurdles; however, how you surpass them makes all the difference. Some things I learned from this experience are:

Ask questions; don't be afraid. If you do not comprehend a financial term or concept, ask your loan officer to explain it simply.

Do not hurry up. Carefully look at the terms and conditions before signing a loan agreement. Be ready for unexpected difficulties.

Stay patient and focused because delays and hitches are part of the loan process. Consider seeking the services of a financial advisor or mentor to help you go through the journey of applying for a loan.

To sum up, getting funding from a national bank was an invaluable experience when I learned about patience, persistence, and being financially literate. It was challenging, but the result was improved skills in dealing with money matters and running my business.

***

Lessons Learned: Navigating the Complexities of Financing and Debt Management

Obtaining funding for my real estate venture was challenging but fruitful. This experience taught me essential lessons regarding financing complexities, debt management intricacies, and how to maneuver through them confidently.

Among the most significant things I got was an emphasis on financial literacy. As a property investor, I used to think about asset values and rental yields. Still, I have never really come across concepts of finance like interest rates, amortization schedules, or collateral.

To overcome this challenge, I taught myself financial concepts and terminologies. I read books on finance and attended seminars on financial aspects of real estate investments, among others. Whenever something wasn't clear to me during these events, I always asked questions. This helped provide me with a good financial foundation that was useful when it came to negotiating better loan terms and managing my debts effectively.

Furthermore, another important lesson from the experience is that one needs a lot of patience and perseverance. It takes quite a long time to secure credit from any national bank. The process involves lots of paperwork, research, and negotiation. However, by being patient and persistent, I managed to get faith that would suit me in all aspects and give me the capital necessary for business growth.

Another lesson learned was the essence of establishing rapport with loaners. By having a good relationship with my credit officer, I was offered a loan at better terms and was given more personalized service. This means that I kept in touch with my bank manager, kept him up-to-date on my business activities, and turned to him whenever any challenges or questions arose.

In addition to these lessons, I learned the importance of effective debt management. Debt is inevitable in the real estate investment business. Poorly handled debt can ruin you financially, just like it happened to me.

I tried not to be caught up in this situation by ensuring that I paid off the high-interest loans, made timely payments, and avoided unnecessary debts. Additionally, I ensured enough cash reserve to handle unexpected expenses or downturns in the market.

Another crucial lesson learned was about the diversification of financing sources. National banks are not the only alternative sources of funds that may exist in town. I also learned about a few other sources of funds that I could have resorted to if I had not used the traditional method of borrowing from banks. Consequently, this enabled me to attract more financing options and negotiate better terms.

Finally, I realized the significance of being adaptable and flexible. The financial market is never static; what works today might not work tomorrow. By keeping an open mind for new ideas and approaches, I stayed ahead of my competitors and adjusted to variations in market forces.

In conclusion, getting funding for my real estate business was challenging yet satisfying. It taught me essential aspects of financial literacy, patience, perseverance, relationship building, debt management skills, diversification, and adaptability. These lessons helped me grow a stronger business and achieve my financial objectives. For every aspiring real estate investor, whether young or old, these lessons can guide you confidently when dealing with debt management and financing complexities.

***

Overcoming Obstacles: Achieving Success in Real Estate Investing

I had a firm resolve to build a flourishing real estate investment portfolio, although obtaining finances and managing debts were difficult. Even though my financing was challenging and involved debt accumulation, I embarked on the journey. As a result of this tenacity, coupled with hard work, I jumped over hurdles and bought several houses in no time.

In retrospect, my success depended on the fact that I was determined. I didn't give up, not even when people rejected me or whenever something went wrong. Thus, I bulldozed ahead with the dream to create a profitable real estate company.

The lack of the right properties proved one of my most important challenges. Being a new investor meant no contacts or knowledge about these markets beyond what is found in textbooks. However, these challenges did not stop me from trying out other alternatives. This means endless hours spent online researching to find homes that are available for sale, attending open house events, and driving around different neighborhoods looking for ideal properties.

Financing posed another challenge for me, too. Getting loans from national banks is complicated and time-consuming, as stated before. Nevertheless, this couldn't prevent me from going forward with my business idea by borrowing ideas such as alternative forms of finance like working with private lenders and negotiating with sellers.

But all odds notwithstanding, I remained focused on achieving my goal. I strove unceasingly to establish my own business. I would often work twelve hours a day, seven days a week. In the process, I lost time that should have been spent with family and friends, and my social life was suspended. Yet I knew it would all be worth it in the end.

And then it happened. It was a moment of pure exhilaration; I had just closed on my first investment, an apartment building in an up-and-coming neighborhood. The joy of this moment could only be matched by the sheer hard work that had brought me here. I took chances, and they paid off.

But I didn't stop there! Consequently, I kept working hard and increasing my real estate holdings. Each step taught me something new about strategy optimization and how to change market conditions. And every property acquired only made me more confident.

Today, I am glad that my attempts at real estate business succeeded. These deals resulted in multiple properties being owned, huge cash flow generated from them, and leaving a legacy for myself and future generations. I cannot truly express this feeling, but it is a mingling of pride, satisfaction, and relief.

If there is one thing an aspiring real estate investor must understand, it is never giving up. The road to success is not smooth; still, it's worth taking. Remain concentrated, determined, and devoted to your target. Let no barriers hinder you nor fear risking.

In conclusion, my path toward success in real estate investment involved various hurdles. But through determination, hard work, and endurance. And achieve my goals. I hope my story inspires and motivates others to pursue their dreams and never give up on their vision of success.

Chapter 8: Learning Through Action

When I first started, I was on HUD, food stamps, and welfare, taking care of my mother in my apartment after the doctors told us there was nothing more they could do for her. My journey began during a challenging period in my life. With four siblings, it was suggested she go to a nursing home, but I chose to keep her with me. At the time, my brother and sisters had good jobs; they couldn't manage to care for her while working, and I couldn't let her stay in the nursing home.

I was at a point in time when I was raising two young boys alone without any support and barely making ends meet. My effort and God's guidance enabled me to succeed later in life after facing tumultuous challenges alone.

When my mother passed away, her house, which still had a mortgage, became a new challenge. My brother asked if I wanted to buy her house, and despite having nothing, I agreed. Shortly after, I received a letter informing me that I had been laid off from General Motors after five years. Fortunately, I found work and started paying off the mortgage on my mother's house.

Years later, my brother asked if I wanted to buy his house too. Initially, I didn't want to because I already had my mother's house. But then it clicked - I could rent it out. I put a rental sign in the window and rented it to a woman who unfortunately didn't take care of the property and it soon became infested with fleas. The situation was so dire that it scared me. Despite my instructions, she had kept pets in the house. Not knowing what to do, the neighbors approached me, asking if I wanted to sell the house. Without any experience in selling property, I agreed. Around the same time, an older gentleman in the neighborhood, whose wife had recently passed away, asked if I wanted to buy his house. I said yes, even though the West Side wasn't suitable to purchase.

I started this business on my own, without any partners. It was a chaotic start, but I continued buying houses. National Bank worked with me with no credit, though they charged high interest rates. I believe that God started me on this path because I chose to care for my mother. After her passing, I dedicated my life to Jesus, and three years later, everything started falling into place. Eventually, I did have a partner who helped me, but the initial drive and decision to venture into real estate were entirely mine.

After my mother died and I bought my mother's house, I always managed to have something. I went to college for a year and a half and got that money. Even though I had to pay it back, I always managed to have something.

My Method for Remodeling Properties

Instead of just purchasing and selling, I remodeled houses to draw new tenants. Making a place people desire to call home is more important than just the location or the cost.

My strategy is focused on improving each home's appearance and usability. In my opinion, a well-designed property can significantly impact drawing in tenants. I want people to feel at home and like they belong as soon as they walk in.

I begin by evaluating the property's advantages and disadvantages.

What are the best aspects of it?

What should be made better?

I develop a vision for the property in collaboration with contractors and designers. Our goal is to update the area without sacrificing its unique character.

Knowing what tenants desire is one of the most important components of my strategy. I've had numerous conversations with prospective customers and discovered that they seek more than simply a place to live. They desire a room that is aesthetically beautiful, cozy, and useful.

To do this, I design light-filled, spacious areas ideal for partying or unwinding. To make tenants' lives easier, I install contemporary appliances, upgrade the electrical and plumbing systems, and add smart home features. I also focus on the details, such as outside spaces, natural light, and storage spaces.

The Ability to Adapt

I've learned from this trip how crucial it is to adapt to new challenges. I've developed the flexibility to adjust my approach to different situations, such as changing customer preferences, unanticipated building delays, or shifts in industry trends.

Accepting challenges has kept me one step ahead of the competition and aided my professional and personal growth. I never would have guessed that I would have become more resourceful and resilient.

Looking back on my experiences, I see that overcoming obstacles and picking up new skills via experience make learning by doing not only a business approach but a way of life. It's about accepting ambiguity, keeping an open mind, and never stopping learning. By sharing my experience, I want to spread it to other people.

***

My Journey to Creating Attractive Rental Properties

When I consider my journey, it makes me think of everything I've learned in the past. Among the most important lessons learned is how crucial it is to make your properties attractive to attract tenants and increase revenue. It has been a road full of trial and error, but in the end, it has helped me create a set of tactics that have consistently been successful.

The Influence of Initial Views

Initial impressions are crucial when renting out a house. A prospective tenant is assessing the space from the moment they walk in. For this reason, it's vital to establish a positive impression immediately. Painting the walls is one of the easiest yet most efficient ways to accomplish this. A new paint job may change a room, giving it a contemporary, tidy, and welcoming appearance.

Installing new fixtures is another important method that I have learned. A property might appear run-down and outdated with outdated hardware, faucets, and lights. You can immediately improve the area and attract potential tenants by swapping outdated fixtures for sleek, contemporary ones.

The Significance of Hygiene

Another essential component of designing a desirable rental property is cleanliness. An untidy or messy place may greatly turn off potential tenants. For this reason, before I show a house to a client, I clean and organize it completely. Every surface, including the counters and flooring, should be glossy and brilliant.

Above and Beyond the Fundamentals

Painting, updating the fixtures, and keeping your rental home clean are all important, but other tactics can make a difference. For instance, incorporating greenery into the area might increase its cozy and pleasant vibe. To give the house some character, I also like to add some artistic accents like carpets or artwork.

Attempt and Error

I didn't immediately pick up all of these strategies, of course. It has taken years of trial and error to determine what works and what doesn't. All of my mistakes have taught me something valuable along the road.

Although I was a big proponent of curb appeal, I didn't initially realize how important it was.

I used to be so interested in the inside of the property that I would overlook its exterior. However, I soon realized that the exterior of the households has equal significance to the interior. A fresh coat of paint on the outside, eye-catching patio furniture, and well-maintained lawns can all help attract tenants.

Increasing Revenue

I've discovered from my experiences that making a rental property appealing requires more than just making it seem good—it also requires optimizing its profit potential. You can raise the property's worth and draw in higher-paying tenants by making the appropriate refurbishment and amenity investments. Achieving the ideal balance between making property investments and controlling expenses has been crucial to success. Maintaining this balance is essential to optimizing profitability, but it's not easy.

Looking back on my voyage, I'm pleased with my accomplishments. I've discovered that designing appealing rental houses is about giving tenants a cozy and inviting atmosphere, not only about turning a profit quickly. Using these techniques, I've built properties that benefit residents and are financially successful.

Chapter 9: Setting Boundaries and Expectations

In my journey as a property owner, I quickly learned that setting boundaries is critical when dealing with tenants. Establishing clear limits and following them protects my financial interests and guarantees a respectful and specialized relationship with the tenants.

Initially, I was often lenient, driven by compassion and a desire to help those who needed housing. I believed flexibility was the correct method, especially when tenants faced financial difficulties or personal hardships. Yet, this leniency sometimes led to challenges, such as delayed payments, property damage, or impractical demands.

I realized that I was risking my financial stability and carelessly allowing unjustifiable behaviors without establishing clear boundaries. Early on, my leniency led to challenges like delayed payments and property damage, highlighting the need for clear and firm guidelines. From the beginning, setting firm, clear prospects became essential for maintaining order and fairness.

I had to clearly outline rent payment deadlines, maintenance responsibilities, and acceptable property use to avoid misunderstandings and ensure everyone knew their roles. This approach wasn't harsh or uncaring; it was about ensuring the tenants, and I understood our responsibilities and obligations. By doing so, I could create a more predictable and manageable setting, reducing the risk of conflicts and ensuring that my properties were maintained properly.

For example, I established strict strategies on rent payment deadlines, maintenance responsibilities, and property use. I communicated these rules to every tenant, leaving no room for mistakes or oversights. Over time, I noticed that this clarity helped prevent unnecessary battles, late rent payments, and misunderstandings, creating a more predictable and manageable environment for everyone involved.

Sticking to these boundaries was sometimes problematic. There were moments when tenants asked for exceptions due to unforeseen situations. While I remained empathetic, I quickly learned to assess each situation carefully and decide whether making an exception was justified or unnecessary. Maintaining consistency with the established rules was essential in many cases to avoid setting a precedent that could lead to further issues.

Enforcing these boundaries also taught me the importance of balancing my sense of compassion with professionalism. While I wanted to help, I also needed to ensure that my business remained feasible in the long run. This meant that sometimes I would have to make tough discussions or make difficult choices, such as evicting tenants who repeatedly violated the terms of their lease or enforcing fines. These decisions were never easy, but they were essential to protect my investments and maintain a fair living environment for other tenants. Setting and obeying these boundaries created a more structured and predictable management process. It freed me up to concentrate on expanding my real estate holdings and offering high-quality rentals instead of being sidetracked by avoidable problems. Eventually, this approach contributed to my personal and specialized growth, reinforcing the importance of clear communication and firm boundaries in any business relationship.

Setting boundaries with tenants is essential, but the decision-making process is equally important when they can't afford to pay rent or deposits. This situation often put me in a tough position, torn between sympathy and the need to maintain the boundaries I had placed to ensure economic stability. I relied deeply on my instincts to guide my decisions in these moments.

When faced with tenants who couldn't afford rent or deposits, my first instinct was often to show compassion. I understood what it was like to struggle financially and wanted to give others the chance to get back on their feet. However, I swiftly learned that while kindness is essential, it cannot come at the expense of my financial well-being. Allowing tenants to stay without paying what was due might have felt like the right thing to do at the moment, but it could lead to long-term financial stress on my business.

I had to learn to evaluate each situation carefully. I might arrange a payment plan or extend the lease if a tenant had a setback. However, I would have to make the difficult choice to uphold the lease conditions if it became evident that they were unwilling or unable to pay. This had nothing to do with being harsh; instead, it was about protecting my company's finances so that I could keep providing accommodation for other people.

I eventually became proficient at seeing the red flags suggested when a renter cannot pay rent. I learned to trust my senses when something didn't feel right. Tenants who routinely missed payments or acted deceptively when discussing their financial situation were frequently warning signs of more significant issues on the road. In those circumstances, I had to constantly remind myself that addressing issues early rather than letting them spiral out of hand was preferable.

I had to weigh the practicalities of managing a real estate company against my desire to lend a hand to maintain my financial stability. Though it wasn't always simple, I understood that in the long run, I needed to safeguard my savings to keep assisting others. This meant that there were moments when I had to make tough decisions against my better judgment.

Negotiating with tenants and applying rental agreements were crucial for managing my properties and protecting my investments. Early in my journey, I realized that clear communication and firm agreements were essential to maintaining order and ensuring my properties remained a viable source of income.

Negotiations often start with setting clear expectations. Being upfront about terms, responsibilities, and consequences helped prevent misunderstandings and disputes. For example, handling payment plans when tenants faced financial difficulties required careful assessment of their history and potential impact on my finances. Balancing compassion with financial stability meant making tough decisions about accepting or rejecting payment plans.

Imposing rental agreements was essential for safeguarding my investments and ensuring the smooth operation of my property management. Reliable enforcement meant that tenants were clear about the importance of following the terms of their lease.

This involved addressing various issues, such as late payments, which could disrupt the financial flow of my business. Moreover, managing property damage was crucial, as any neglect or harm to the property could impact its value and rental income. Compliance with all lease terms was also a significant enforcement aspect, ensuring tenants adhered to property use and maintenance rules.

In some cases, enforcing these agreements required taking legal action. For example, eviction proceedings became necessary if tenants repeatedly violated lease terms or failed to meet their financial duties despite repeated warnings. While initiating legal action was always a last resort, it was sometimes crucial for protecting my property and maintaining financial stability. Such measures ensured that I could uphold the truth of my rental agreements and maintain a fair and orderly rental environment. These experiences taught me that negotiating and enforcing agreements were not just about control but also about creating a fair rental environment. Balancing firmness with empathy helped me manage tenant relationships while securing my investments.

My journey has taught me valuable lessons about firmly handling difficult situations and enforcing policies. Dealing with challenging situations often requires a blend of determination and flexibility. When faced with issues like late payments or tenant disputes, I learned the importance of staying composed and addressing problems directly. For instance, when tenants failed to meet their payment obligations or dishonored lease terms, it was crucial to act promptly and decisively. This involved clear communication about expectations and the consequences of non-compliance.

Implementing policies consistently was essential for maintaining order and ensuring all tenants understood their responsibilities. Setting clear, written policies from the beginning helped ease misunderstandings and disputes. Upholding these policies required a firm stance, even when it was uncomfortable. This might include issuing formal warnings, applying late fees, or taking legal action if necessary.

Although it wasn't always simple, maintaining my ground in these circumstances was essential to safeguarding my investments and ensuring my property management business ran well. I maintained standards and gave each tenant a stable atmosphere by unwittingly enforcing the policies. These experiences have taught me that aggressiveness and empathy must be balanced to handle challenging circumstances and implement policies. This strategy protects your interests while preserving a just and organized renting environment.

Chapter 10: Empowering Others, Empowering Myself

My journey from poverty to property ownership wasn't straightforward. It was filled with trials and learning experiences that made me who I am today. Through it all, my resilience grew as I faced and overcame various difficulties.

When I first started buying houses, my financial situation was very incomplete. I was on a tight budget, so I had to be very practical. I took on several repairs and maintenance tasks myself to save money. This included painting walls, fixing leaks, and handling various repairs. Since I was involved with HUD (the Housing and Urban Development program), I had to ensure that my properties met their strict standards.

This often meant dealing with long lists of requirements, sometimes up to ten or fifteen items, even if I had already addressed some. The demands were frequent and occasionally redundant, creating a continuous struggle. Despite these challenges, I adapted by learning new skills and finding efficient ways to complete tasks. I remained persistent, focusing on maintaining the properties and meeting the HUD standards, which helped me manage through those tough early days. Resilience played a significant role in my journey. It wasn't about having a grand plan or approach but rather about having the mindset to grab opportunities as they came. When I started with my first properties, I didn't know what I could do. It was a learning procedure, figuring things out as I went along. I just knew I wanted something better, and I took every chance that came my way.

Helping others was not my original goal when I began buying properties. My primary intention was to secure a stable income and improve my living conditions. At the outset, I focused on making a living and gradually improving my financial situation. As I acquired more properties, I started renting them out, which unintentionally led me to help others by providing them a place to live. This shift in focus came from my experiences and understanding of what it feels like to struggle.

I realized that everyone deserves a chance to have a safe and comfortable home, which motivated me to continue offering housing opportunities. Even though not all tenants appreciated the effort and resources I invested into maintaining the properties, I remained committed to this approach. I knew that providing housing was not just about the financial aspects but about doing the right thing and allowing people to live in a decent environment.

Maintaining the properties and dealing with ungrateful tenants were challenging, but my commitment to helping others remained steadfast. I understood that even if the appreciation wasn't always visible, the impact of providing a stable home was significant for those in need. This realization kept me going, reinforcing my belief that continuing to offer homes was an essential and worthwhile effort despite the difficulties. Financially, my journey required careful planning and resourcefulness. I took out small loans to start, understanding that these initial steps were crucial for setting up my property business. I was strategic about using these loans, ensuring that every bit of money I earned was reinvested into acquiring additional properties. National Bank played a significant role in this phase despite the high interest rates they charged. Their support was vital for my growth, even though it meant dealing with higher costs.

I meticulously managed my finances and reinvested profits to expand my property portfolio steadily. Each property purchase was a calculated move aimed at gradually building my wealth. Over time, this approach helped me achieve a stable financial foundation, reflecting my incremental progress through diligent effort and strategic investment.

One of the ways I aimed to make a positive impact was by offering housing opportunities without requiring large deposits. I recognized that many people were stressed financially and might find it challenging to gather the upfront costs typically required to secure a rental property. By waiving the deposit, I planned to ease this burden and provide an opportunity for those in desperate need of stable housing.

I hoped this approach would help people find a place to live and offer them a fresh start without the added stress of spending a substantial amount of money upfront. My goal was to create an environment where people could secure a home even if they were facing financial problems, thereby giving them a chance to stabilize their lives and recover from their situation.

Dealing with renters who moved in without the appropriate deposit money presented me with great difficulties. Many of them promised to pay their deposits later and would eventually come up with excuses for being unable to pay. Some would say they needed just a few more weeks, only to delay even further with stories of family emergencies or other unexpected expenses. Major issues arose with younger tenants who sometimes exploited my flexibility.

This repeated pattern of excuses and delayed payments created significant frustration and financial strain. Despite these difficulties and the often unfulfilled promises, I continued offering leniency. My decision was driven by a deep belief in giving people a chance to secure housing, even when my efforts were not always valued or reciprocated. Despite the challenges, this pledge to help others reflected my dedication to providing opportunities and support for those in need.

Reflecting on my journey, I realize that my experiences with renting and upholding properties were as much about personal growth as they were about economic gain. They taught me resilience and persistence. Kindness and leniency with tenants didn't always yield positive results. Sometimes, a firm stance was necessary to protect my reserves.

Eventually, giving affordable housing to others served to fulfill my sense of purpose and need. The lessons I learned, and the resilience I developed through these experiences have shaped my approach to life and my understanding of what it means to help others truly.

These experiences taught me a lot about resilience and the difficulties of balancing kindness with business realities. They highlighted the problems of offering support while ensuring financial stability. It reinforced the importance of careful tenant screening and setting clear expectations to alleviate some of these issues.

While the challenges were numerous and sometimes discouraging, they provided valuable lessons about managing empathy and practicality. Each experience contributed to my growth and understanding of directing the fine line between offering assistance and maintaining a sustainable business.

Despite the obstacles, I found thoughtful fulfillment in my efforts to empower others. Even under difficult conditions, providing housing opportunities allowed me to contribute positively to people's lives. By offering homes to those in need, I helped them create a stable environment, which gave me a sense of purpose and success.

Balancing compassion with the demands of property management was not always easy. However, each challenge was a learning experience that helped me grow stronger and more resilient. The difficulties I met with tenants and the struggles of maintaining properties taught me invaluable lessons about perseverance and setting boundaries.

Amidst these trials, I also saw significant developments in my financial situation. As I continued to manage and invest in properties, I built my wealth and achieved a level of financial stability that was once out of reach. This economic growth was a personal victory and a reflection of the hard work and dedication I poured into my business.

Finally, empowering others while improving my circumstances provided a fulfillment that exceeded monetary advantages. It was about recognizing that, despite the difficulties, my efforts were having a beneficial effect on the community.

Helping others and becoming financially successful together demonstrated how personal development and career success may exist together. This period showed me that genuine empowerment is about supporting others and finding courage and fulfillment along the way.

Chapter 11: Dealing with Deception

Managing deception from renters, especially when it's time to pay, is one of the more challenging components of property management. It is possible that despite your best efforts, your tenant proves to be dishonest. I have seen more than my fair share of cases where renters used various deceptive methods to get out of paying their dues or following their leases.

For example, some tenants make elaborate promises during the initial rental discussions, only to later use excuses like claiming the mailman lost their check or fabricating family emergencies to delay or avoid payments.

One case that stands out in my memory involved a tenant who initially seemed very eager and reliable. He was keen to move into a property left in disarray by the previous tenant. I set some clear conditions for his move-in: he needed to clean the property, paint the rooms, and handle other necessary maintenance tasks. Despite his willingness and ready promises, he eventually became unresponsive when discussing rent and the deposit. He even went so far as to change his phone number without notifying me, illustrating a classic avoidance tactic.

These deceptive practices tested my patience and made me realize the need to stay alert and think carefully. Dealing with situations like these meant being firm but fair. I learned to spot warning signs early on, like when a tenant's communication didn't add up, or their promises seemed too good to be true. I also realized the importance of taking quick action when faced with dishonesty. The longer you let them get away with it, the more they'll take advantage of it. Like they say, "You give them an inch, they'll take a mile." Yet, each experience with a tricky tenant taught me how to handle things better and protect my interests as a property manager. But it wasn't as easy when I was still new and learning the ropes.

As the weeks passed, the situation with the tenant, who avoided all contact with me, got worse. By the end of the second month, I tried to reach him to sort out the rent and deposit, but he was impossible to find. No matter how many times I tried, he wouldn't respond. I eventually contacted his cousin, who told me he had changed his phone number without telling me.

When I finally contacted him using a different phone, he said, "I'm not paying you anything."

It was clear that this tenant was deeply dishonest. He agreed to do specific tasks but refused to pay rent, revealing his true intentions. When this happened, I decided to take him to court. Even then, he didn't show up, but the judge ruled in my favor. The court gave him a week to leave the property and ordered him to pay me $4,000. This money helped cover my expenses because of his actions and the cleanup needed after the previous tenant.

This experience taught me that not everyone keeps promises or acts in good faith. It's imperative to notice warning signs early and take action quickly when dealing with dishonest tenants. In the following sections, I'll share how to recognize when a tenant is lying, identify common warning signs, and discuss strategies to handle deception in property management.

Dealing with tenants who are good at misleading others can be very tricky. These smooth talkers can grab your attention and convince you with their words, making it difficult to discern between fact and fiction. I've had tenants in the past who were quite adept at talking their way out of many issues. Their stories were often detailed and seemed believable at first.

For example, one tenant might tell a long, emotional story about a family emergency that drained their account, causing issues with paying rent on time. Understanding their predicament, I'd happily give them an extension. But this would happen repeatedly – they'd use similar excuses monthly.

Then, there's another trick – the tenant might convincingly claim that they're waiting for a check to clear that's delayed. Again, that's a perfectly understandable situation that can make you feel sympathetic and offer them more time to pay, as they're unsure about what to do next. In normal circumstances, the tenant would make the payment soon after. But, in this case, the check never clears.

Dealing with such smooth talkers in property management means staying grounded and not letting their charm affect your judgment. From my experience, these tenants can be very persuasive, telling stories that seem believable or that pull at your emotions. But I've learned that you can't just trust their words; you need solid evidence and consistent actions to make such decisions. It's easy to be swayed if they seem honest, but the more convincing they are, the more cautious you should be. These stories often just buy them time or help them avoid their responsibilities.

To protect myself and my property, I always check if what the tenant says is true. If they claim they've mailed a check to me, I ask for a tracking number or proof of payment. I ask for supporting documents to verify their claim if they mention a family emergency. The goal is to ensure you're not being taken advantage of. It is not about not believing people. People who are genuinely facing difficulties will, in my experience, recognize the need to provide evidence to back up their claims. On the other hand, dishonest people may become defensive or attempt to alter their story when questioned about it.

Another significant strategy is to set clear rules and boundaries from the beginning. I always ensure the whole thing is written out in the lease agreement, with payment deadlines, maintenance responsibilities, and what happens if they don't obey the rules. If a tenant tries to make justifications, I refer back to the lease and remind them of their agreement. Even if I'm ready to hear their concerns, this approach shows that I take the regulations seriously.

Ultimately, the key to handling these difficult situations has been remaining grounded and concentrating on the facts rather than becoming drawn into someone else's perspective.

It all comes down to striking the correct balance between safeguarding and comprehending your assets and ensuring that someone isn't taking advantage of you.

Tips for Recognizing and Handling Deception

Here are some easy suggestions for handling dishonesty in landlord-tenant interactions based on my experiences:

1. **Look for Red Flags:** Pay attention to inconsistencies in what a tenant says or does. If they promise to send a check and it doesn't show up, or they have frequent last-minute emergencies affecting their ability to pay the rent, these could be signs they're not being truthful. Watch for patterns that suggest they might be lying.

2. **Set Clear Potentials:** Be clear about what you expect from the start. Ensure your lease contract covers payment terms, maintenance duties, and what happens if rules are broken. Clear guidelines help avoid confusion and allow you to act if problems arise.

3. **Communicate in Writing:** Always use official channels for communication. Ask for written proof or documentation if a tenant says they've sent a check or have an issue. This way, you have a record of all connections and agreements.

4. **Confirm Their Claims:** Don't just take a tenant's word for things. If they give excuses or clarifications,

ask for evidence. For example, ask for supporting documents if they mention a family emergency.

5. **Apply the Lease:** Be firm but fair in sticking to the lease terms. If a tenant is often late with payments or not fulfilling their duties, take action according to the tenancy agreement. This might include giving formal warnings, charging late fees, or seeking legal help.

6. **Get Legal Advice:** Consult a legal expert if you suspect severe dishonesty or have ongoing problems. They can guide you on the right steps and ensure you follow proper legal measures.

By closely monitoring and following these strategies, you can better manage complicated situations with tenants and protect your interests. Being fair yet cautious will help you handle these encounters more efficiently.

Chapter 12: Navigating Personal and Professional Challenges

Over the years, being a landlord has put me in many emotionally and professionally tough situations. I faced challenges managing properties and testing how strong and resourceful I could be. They made me examine how well I could handle these complex problems and deal with stress. Many of the issues I faced mixed my personal life with my work in ways I had not planned for.

For example, when dealing with tenants who caused trouble or when I handled repairs while coping with personal problems, I realized that it required me to balance both sides of my life carefully. This balancing act was often tricky, and it made me realize how important it was to manage my feelings and professional duties with a degree of mindfulness.

Being honest and explicit about my obligations to my tenants was one of the first things I learned to do as a landlord. I was pretty clear from the beginning that covering utilities like gas, heat, electricity, and rent were constant commitments on the tenants' part.

I often told my tenants, "You can eat beans for the rest of the week if you don't have money, but you have to face your responsibilities."

This method worked well in most cases since it established a clear understanding between me and my tenants. However, as I would soon learn, when dealing with someone who doesn't want to pay, even the best-laid plans can be disrupted by unpredictable conditions.

Once, I came upon a tenant who failed to pay her rent. When I approached her about it, she got mad, making it one of the most awful experiences I have ever had. I had called her numerous times to get through to her, but she never replied. Worried and dissatisfied with this lack of communication, I visited her. I dropped by and saw that her apartment door was unlocked when I arrived, and I could hear her inside. I called out to her and knocked, but she didn't answer.

After a while, when it was clear that I wouldn't go away, she appeared arrogant and hostile. The discussion quickly turned into an argument where she was attacking me with an intensity that took me by surprise. I was suddenly overcome with fear.

I became aware of my vulnerability as I stood there in front of a much stronger and bigger woman than I was. Considering that I was about to get into a physical altercation over a dispute for unpaid rent in my role as a landlord was unnerving. I hadn't been in one since I was eighteen, and I wasn't about to change that. I had no other option but to back down and call the police, who suggested that I file a lawsuit. This event served as a sobering reminder of how easily things may get out of hand and how crucial it was to take precautions and be mindful.

Apart from managing uncooperative renters, I also faced various difficulties with the upkeep and maintenance of the property. I remember one specific occasion very clearly. After the previous renter had walked out, they left the place in horrifying shape. A survey of the place revealed general damages, holes in the walls, and even Kool-Aid stains on the floors. The destruction was astonishing, and I knew it would need much money and effort to repair the property and regain its usable state.

First, I had the damages fixed by a handyman. But rather than making things better, he only made them worse. He was so careless that paint spilled on the carpet, and made other careless mistakes while working, which only worsened the situation. I was so angry and felt let down that I had to ask my now-husband, who was once my fiancé, for assistance.

Despite his work obligations, he gladly helped to clean up the mess. Together, we had to fix the walls, replace the carpet, and redo much of the poorly done work. This event served as an expensive reminder of the risks of taking shortcuts and the value of hiring qualified assistance.

These incidents brought home many lessons and showed me how difficult it was to manage rental homes while still fulfilling my commitments as a landlord. I frequently felt that these obligations were too much to bear, and I had difficulty managing them. But, I had to learn how to handle personal issues and the duties of being a landlord simultaneously.

I remember when a close family member passed away during one of the most challenging times I had as a landlord. I was overcome with grief, yet I had to keep going about my business. The properties needed continuous care, and the tenants still had problems that needed to be fixed. One particular tenant during this period caused me additional worry by abandoning the property in a poor shape that required expensive repairs.

In addition to managing his work obligations, my fiancé stepped in to help clean up the mess at the assets. Even though I was thankful for his help, it was unsatisfying. He had his tasks, meaning the repairs took longer than I wanted. But I had to accept that despite all my hard work, I couldn't control everything. I had to learn to be patient, trust that things would eventually get sorted out, and understand that sometimes, even good help isn't available immediately. This practice showed me that I needed to keep pushing forward and not let setbacks get me down.

It took a heavy emotional toll on me to juggle my work and personal obligations during this trying period. It was draining to constantly be under pressure to manage the finances, take care of the homes, and deal with the tenant's difficulties while grieving. I felt like I could hardly stand up on certain days, and the pressure was getting to me. I couldn't, however, afford to let my feelings delay my work.

Any hint of weakness on the property owner's part could encourage tenants to benefit from the conditions, making things much more complex. I had to dig deep during this time to find the willpower to continue. I established the capability to sort my sadness, putting it aside when I had obligations to appear to. Sometimes, I wanted to give up because it wasn't easy. However, I was aware that my only option was to press on. The company had to continue, and I couldn't afford to let my issues destroy all I had spent so much time and energy building.

This occasion taught me a lot about persistence. I discovered that I was tougher than I had previously believed. Even though it felt like everything was falling apart, I could persist and keep everything in order. This tenacity helped me get through those problematic times and made me a better landlord by preparing me to face any trials. I found that I had the strength to continue, no matter how bad things became.

The importance of establishing restrictions was yet another crucial lesson I learned. It's simple for the errands of your job to take over your life if you're a landlord. Whether managing maintenance, resolving tenant worries, or handling unpredicted costs, something must always be done. But I understood I would burn out if I neglected to care for myself. Setting limits helped me stay well-balanced and ensured I had the energy and concentration to manage my properties properly.

Setting limits meant knowing when to say no and realizing that not every problem needed to be solved immediately. It also meant setting aside time, especially when I had none. I realized I could not fulfill my obligations if I neglected my needs. This realization was a game-changer since it allowed me to approach my work more clearly and objectively. Another important strategy that helped me handle the constant responsibilities of being a landlord was learning to stay prepared. Keeping things in order was crucial for handling the workload and reducing anxiety. To do this, I made lists of what needed to be done, set up clear timetables, and kept thorough records. This way, when surprising problems arose, which happened a lot, I could handle them more easily without feeling too stressed. Being organized helped me stay on top of everything and made the job more controllable.

I created a system, for instance, to keep track of maintenance requests, rent payments, and other matters about tenants. I maintained control over the situation and ensured that nothing was overlooked because of this technique. When a tenant called with a problem, I could quickly look up the information and deal with the matter. This degree of order was essential for handling the work demands and stopping minor issues from becoming major ones.

I also learned how critical it is to ask for help when needed. It's simple to slip into the trap of trusting that you must handle everything yourself as a landlord. However, I soon concluded that attempting to manage everything alone would only lead to exhaustion. I discovered that I didn't have to handle every obstacle by myself, whether it was asking my spouse for assistance with maintenance on the house or seeking legal advice when there were disagreements between tenants. Knowing when to seek assistance and delegate responsibilities when feasible was crucial to manage the workload and lower stress levels. For instance, I occasionally paid experts to perform maintenance or repairs outside my competence. Even though doing this occasionally required spending more money up ahead, I frequently avoided anger and wasted time. In addition, getting legal counsel during tenant disputes made it easier for me to handle challenging circumstances and avoid dangers.

Last, knowing how to relax and recharge was significant for keeping my well-being intact. I understood that making time for simple activities that brought joy and helped me unwind was necessary. Whether taking a quiet walk to clear my mind, spending quality time with my family, or just having a few moments to breathe and reflect, these small acts of self-care made a significant transformation.

They helped me stay strong, particularly during challenging times when everything seemed irresistible. Even when things were chaotic, these moments of peace helped me stay grounded and attentive, reminding me that taking care of myself was just as important as taking care of my responsibilities.

One of the finest approaches I could find to refuel was to get outside and spend time in nature. Whether gardening or walking in the park, I discovered that the outdoors allowed me to gain clarity and relax. I would stroll through the park and listen to the birds and breeze, briefly taking my mind off my difficulties. The indoor plants I nurtured provided me with a sense of peace and grounding. These small moments of reflection helped me regain my energy and return to work with fresh liveliness and clarity.

Another vital part of caring for myself was spending time with my family. Being with my husband, who was always there to sustain me, made me feel more grounded and linked. Whether we were working on a project together or enjoying a quiet evening at home, these moments were crucial for me. They gave me the strength and ease to handle the rough circumstances of being a landlord. My husband's help, especially when things got overwhelming, reminded me that I wasn't alone in facing these tests.

To sum up, renting is a demanding occupation that needs a lot of mental, physical, and expressive energy. However, it is possible to handle these problems and preserve personal well-being simultaneously if the appropriate solutions are implemented. Establishing limits, maintaining organization, getting support, and scheduling self-care activities were all crucial strategies that allowed me to manage work expectations without compromising my well-being.

Chapter 13: The Toll of Tenant Troubles

Over the years, dealing with problematic tenants has been hard on my finances and sentiments. Whenever I had to spend money on upkeep, repairs, and general maintenance, it felt like my resources were exhausted. I worked hard to keep my properties in good shape, ensuring they looked beautiful and welcoming. But watching how some tenants treated these homes was distressing. I understand that most people don't see these places as their own – they are renting, after all, but sometimes, it made me question how they lived.

I felt pressured and exhausted from this relentless cycle where I was constantly having to undo the damage they did. What's worse is that my job felt pretty thankless - the tenants didn't appear to appreciate the work I put in. It also had to do with the fact that tenants only contact landlords when there's a problem. Very rarely do tenants just call to thank you for completing the repairs or sorting out a problem quickly.

I experienced mixed emotions whenever it was time for a tenant to move out. I felt like all my efforts were in vain when I saw the conditions in which they would abandon the locations. It would leave a bad impression and lingering effect on me, even after investing time, money, and care into them. I can clearly say that when weighing the losses, the financial strain was not as great as the emotional cost here.

One of the most painful experiences I had as a landlord involved a tenant who left the property in awful condition. When they moved out, I found the apartment covered in pet waste and trash. The filth in that place was astounding, and I was amazed to see that they lived in such squalor. Or maybe they'd messed up the place badly because they were moving out. Regardless of their motivations, the mess was so bad that it required a lot of cleaning and repairs.

But, what truly broke my heart was that I had worked hard to prepare the apartment, making sure it was clean and welcoming for them when they were just moving in. Seeing it in such a terrible state was disappointing. The extensive cleanup and repairs cost me a lot of money, adding to the stress of managing the property. Each time I faced such circumstances, it felt like a personal letdown despite my best efforts to maintain the home.

Another unsatisfying situation occurred when an evicted tenant didn't return the key to the security door. Because of this, I had to get the locks replaced and spent $250 just for new doorknobs. The tenants did it intentionally because they were upset about being asked to leave. This added unnecessary financial stress on top of the emotional strain of dealing with difficult tenants. Managing rental properties became even more demanding because it wasn't just about the money but also about the frustration and disappointment of constantly facing these problems. These instances were part of a larger trend of monetary loss and psychological pain brought on by careless tenants. With each one that I faced, I became emotionally and financially worried as each new issue felt like an extra burden. One time, I had a tenant who clogged the sink by pouring grease down the drain, which caused a significant plumbing problem. The sink got backed up, flooding the entire basement and overflowing. This basement wasn't just an empty space; I had spent much time and money making it nice. I had it fully equipped, with a shower and a toilet installed to be a relaxing area. But after the flooding, the whole place was ruined. Water was everywhere, and the damage was so bad that it felt like all my hard work had been exploited.

What made things worse was that the tenant wouldn't admit their fault or accept that they were accountable. They acted like it wasn't their fault, so I had to handle the entire cost of repairs myself. It was frustrating to not only deal with the physical mess but also to be stuck with the bill, knowing that it all could have been avoided if they had just taken better care of the place. The financial burden was heavy, but the emotional toll of seeing something I had put so much effort into get devastated was just as difficult.

This type of situation was not exceptional. I frequently met tenants who left the properties occupied in far worse condition than what they were given - flooded rooms, spoiled walls, and ruined carpets requiring extensive repairs were the norm. And all of it was handled at my own expense. Each tenant's departure involved cleaning, fixing, and spending money to restore the property to living conditions.

Frustration only worsened when some tenants acted like everything should be handed to them. They would demand repairs and maintenance but wouldn't want to pay for anything or admit their role in causing the difficulties. It didn't matter how much damage they caused, whether it was their fault or not; they always expected me to take care of it for free. They never took accountability for their actions, which added to the emotional and financial stress of being a landlord. Every new issue meant more money out of my pocket, and the lack of esteem from the tenants made it even harder to deal with.

I dedicated much time, energy, and money to ensure the homes I rented were more than just basic living places. I didn't stop at the minimum; I always tried to go the extra mile. Whether upgrading appliances, repainting walls, or installing new flooring, I wanted my tenants to feel like they were moving into a real home, not just a rental property. I made sure everything was fresh, organized, and in great condition. It was important to me that when people walked in, they felt welcomed and relaxed, like they were stepping into a place they could truly call home.

My regular collection of overdue rent and implementation of rental agreements often led to tenant struggles. Despite my efforts to be fair and empathetic, many tenants viewed me as the "bad guy." This was one of the toughest aspects of being a landlord. I wasn't running a charity; I had bills and monetary responsibilities. It was particularly tough when I had to remind tenants to pay their rent or follow the terms of their lease. They often reacted as if I was being unfair or irrational. In several instances, tenants failed to pay their rent, and when I had no choice but to ask them to leave, they blamed me for the situation. This blame game added to the stress and hindrance of managing rental properties. Despite my attempts to work with them, their absence of responsibility and tendency to shift the blame onto others made my role even more difficult.

In some situations, tenants would completely stop cooperating with me. They would ignore my efforts to fix difficulties and refuse to return the keys after the eviction, making everything more complex. This lack of cooperation often meant I had to deal with the extra headache of changing locks or dealing with other issues.

Apart from that, there were also cases where tenants would intentionally harm the property to get even for upholding the lease terms. To retaliate against me for asking them to leave or demanding servicing, they might, for instance, abandon unclean carpets or damaged fixtures. This behavior was petty and annoying and required me to spend extra time and money on repairs and replacements.

This pattern of irresponsible behavior from tenants was something I encountered frequently. It felt like a new wave of stress and financial strain each time. It exhausted my energy and took a significant toll on my resources, making managing properties even more challenging. Even when I genuinely tried to be patient and understanding, offering tenants multiple chances to catch up on overdue rent or address issues, I often seemed the bad guy. I tried to be flexible and work with them, but many tenants interpreted my need to enforce basic rental rules as a personal slight. They tried to be kind and forgiving, but they didn't seem to understand that I was responsible for my expenses, including bills and maintenance, and that running a rental property is a business.

I had to be professional, forceful, and composed when dealing with challenging tenants, especially during tense situations. As time passed, I discovered that maintaining composure was essential to handling these circumstances well. One of the most important strategies I developed was clear communication.

I stayed in touch with tenants regularly, not just when issues arose. As part of this proactive strategy, we followed up to determine if they needed anything or had any problems. By keeping this communication channel open, I could deal with little difficulties before they became significant. For example, if a renter brought up a minor concern as soon as possible, I could set up repairs immediately, keeping it from worsening and costing more money. Using this strategy made managing the properties easier and less stressful when dealing with unforeseen issues.

Establishing firm boundaries was just as vital as listening to my tenants to keep our relationship positive. While I had to maintain a professional demeanor in all dealings, I wanted my tenants to feel comfortable coming to me with any problems. This meant focusing solely on our relationship's lease terms and business aspects. When tenants had issues or complaints, I listened carefully but kept the conversation to the lease terms and any practical solutions. This strategy kept our discussions on topic and helped us avoid misunderstandings by keeping them from getting personal. I wanted to establish an atmosphere where everyone could collaborate well and understand what to expect by keeping things simple and uncomplicated.

It is evident to me that I couldn't do maintenance tasks alone. My then-fiancé, my spouse, first assisted me with the maintenance. We worked together to handle repairs and address issues that came up. I realized I needed additional help as time passed, so I hired a maintenance man.

It was important to me that both my husband and the maintenance man understood how crucial it was to maintain professionalism and respect when dealing with tenants. We aimed to address maintenance concerns promptly to prevent small issues from becoming bigger problems.

Our prompt response to maintenance requests allowed us to address problems before they worsened. However, I also had to ensure the tenants didn't abuse the position and followed the restrictions. This equilibrium preserved excellent ties with the renters and kept everything operating smoothly.

The lesson I learned most from this experience was the need to be fair but forceful. As a property manager, I learned that I had to balance understanding and preventing tenants from taking advantage of me. I learned early on that being overly lenient could cause issues since some tenants might use it as an excuse to avoid their obligations. On the other hand, being overly strict could strain relationships and create unnecessary conflict.

I eventually learned how to establish boundaries and maintain open lines of communication. While I did my best to listen to tenants' complaints and resolve problems, I also upheld the guidelines and standards specified in the lease agreements. Tenants would then know what was expected of them and that I was a fair but firm landlord.

This approach wasn't immediate; it took practice and patience to get it right. But once I found that balance, managing my properties became more manageable. It allowed me to maintain control over my properties and handle tenant issues more effectively while fostering a more respectful and cooperative atmosphere. This balance made the job less stressful and helped keep things running smoothly.

Chapter 14: Taking Back Control

As a landlord, making difficult choices and handling challenging circumstances was frequently necessary to evict troublesome tenants and reclaim control over my properties. There were some crucial things to take into account when making tough decisions.

Dealing with renters who refused to pay their rent or security deposits was one of the biggest obstacles. This wasn't only about the overdue payments; it was a persistent problem. It was about making sure that tenants followed the conditions of the lease, and I was able to regain control over my property. Notably, tenants often didn't return keys because they were angry about being evicted. These tenants frequently appeared to be bitter when asked to pay up and often retaliated in other ways, which added to the difficulty of the procedure.

I often had to take a renter to court to settle disputes arising from late rent payments or lease violations. This was a typical aspect of overseeing and managing rental homes. However, it was not a method that I was a fan of. Instead, if feasible, I made every effort possible to resolve conflicts with the renters politely and directly. For example, when tenants wanted to change the property, I would allow reasonable modifications like painting, provided they adhered to agreed-upon colors. But, there were times when, despite my best attempts to resolve these issues peacefully and amicably, I found myself in court regularly to deal with them. Even then, things didn't pan out as smoothly as I hoped. At times, the tenants would fail to attend court dates, which complicated the process. Their absences only added further delays in the proceedings and increased my stress, turning a straightforward legal issue into a more convoluted, drawn-out and frustrating ordeal. Dealing with these cases in court became a necessary, though unpleasant, part of running my rental properties.

In addition to nonpayment, tenants often ignored other rules, like disregarding the bans on pets. Despite clear policies stating against it, some tenants would still bring pets into the property, causing much damage and making maintenance more difficult. Pets, especially the ones that aren't looked after, can lead to extra wear and tear on the property. I've had to deal with everything from pet owners letting their pets relieve themselves on carpeted floors to not cleaning up their messes or scratch marks on doors, floors, and even the walls, just adding to the maintenance and upkeep workload. One tenant even left a dog tied to a chair, that scratched the walls and caused significant damage.

When tenants disregarded clearly defined rules, taking decisive action to regain control of the property became necessary. This often meant fining them, and if that didn't work, then I'd have no choice but to initiate the eviction process and see it through to the end to ensure that the property was restored and future violations were prevented. For example, when tenants painted walls with unauthorized colors like dark blue or dark brown on white walls, I had to document the changes, estimate the cost to revert them, and pursue legal action if necessary. My approach remained consistent when dealing with property damage or disruptive behavior. The first step was always thorough documentation. In legal matters, this documentation was vital. I often had to present this evidence in court to recover damages caused by tenants. This included recording minor and major damages like broken glass panes, lost keys, and even Kool-Aid spills on carpets. Documenting every violation and following legal procedures were critical steps in maintaining control and protecting my investment and myself when taking them to court.

Additionally, I started requesting tenants' driving licenses and Social Security numbers for more detailed information, which proved helpful in court for recovering owed money. I also employed the services of a reliable locksmith, Mister Baker, who could open any door even if I didn't have the keys, ensuring I could access the property when necessary.

I also wanted to ensure that the living conditions were up to state-defined standards and my standards. Additionally, to retain control of my properties, I followed a straightforward process each time. This taught me the importance of being firm and consistent in managing rental properties, even though it was often a long and challenging process.

To properly handle the matter, I followed a well-defined method, especially when dealing with property damage and disruptive conduct from tenants:

1. **Documenting the Damage**: Recording all the damage the tenants had caused was the first step. This includes broken glass panes in the windows, lost keys, and wall holes. Additional damages included tearing down ceiling fans and unauthorized painting of dark-colored walls. I needed to keep records of these problems as they aided in my ability to file a dispute, either in court or out of it, and get paid for the necessary repairs. Having a thorough record to support my allegations, especially in court, was crucial.

2. **Filing Claims for Repairs**: Even if I had insurance, there were instances where I had to pay for the repairs after recording the damage. This required figuring out how much it would cost to replace the shattered glass or patch the holes in the walls and the fine that the tenant would incur for damaging the property. In cases where tenants stole appliances like stoves and refrigerators, I had to document these thefts and get the police involved to recover losses. I had to take this action to make sure I could get the renters who caused the damage to pay for the repairs, partially, if not fully.

3. **Taking Legal Action**: There were times when I had to take tenants to court when they were stubborn about clearing their rent or refused to pay for the substantial damage they had caused. In such instances, I was forced to undertake legal action to defend my rights and seek the appropriate compensation. For example, after a tenant moved out and damaged the property, including tearing

down ceiling fans and painting walls without permission, legal action was necessary to recover costs.

4. **Handling Unauthorized Changes**: Unauthorized changes to the property, such as painting walls a color that isn't permitted by the lease, are something that some renters have done. Addressing these issues required going through the same steps: documenting the changes, estimating the cost to undo them, and taking legal action if needed. Tenants often insisted on specific colors like dark blue or dark brown, which required additional effort to restore the property to its original state.

By following these steps, I effectively managed damage and disruptive behavior. This gave me back control over my homes and ensured they were kept up nicely for potential renters.

Keeping up with property standards while managing renters who disregarded guidelines and limits was one of the most challenging aspects of being a landlord. Thinking back on these difficulties reveals the methods I employed to maintain my properties' standards despite tenant infractions.

1. **Enforcing Rules and Boundaries**: Ensuring tenants followed the guidelines outlined in the lease agreement was one of the largest challenges. Even with explicit instructions, some renters would disobey prohibitions, such as bringing pets into a building that does not allow pets or doing unlawful modifications like painting walls. For instance, when tenants ignored the no-pet policy and brought in animals that caused damage, I had to enforce the rules

strictly. This disregard required constant vigilance and enforcement on my part. I had to be firm and consistent in addressing these violations to protect the property's condition.

2. Dealing with Neglect and Damage: Tenants who did not respect property standards often left behind significant damage. This includes carelessness that resulted in more severe problems, such as unclean or broken flooring and fixtures, and physical damage, like holes in the walls. Specific instances included tenants tearing down ceiling fans and painting walls in unauthorized colors, which required substantial repairs. It took a lot of emotional work and money to solve these issues because it demoralized me to watch properties fall apart despite my best efforts to keep them up.

3. Balancing Equality and Firmness: Achieving a balance between fairness and firmness when dealing with tenants was crucial. To stop more harm and uphold property standards, I had to enforce the rules even though I wanted to be sympathetic to their circumstances. Despite understanding tenants' struggles, I had to remain firm, often leading to difficult conversations and eventual evictions. This frequently required having unpleasant discussions and coming to harsh conclusions, such as filing for eviction when tenants consistently disobeyed the regulations.

4. Managing Emotional Stress: Dealing with tenants who did not uphold property standards took a heavy emotional toll. After spending money and effort on upkeep, every instance of damage to the property or breaking the rules felt like a personal slight. Instances like tenants stealing appliances or causing extensive property damage left me feeling emotionally drained and frustrated. It was a daily struggle to handle the stress of these problems and keep a professional appearance.

5. **Implementing Preventive Measures**: I implemented preventive measures like careful tenant screenings and transparent property rule communication to lessen these difficulties. I tried to reduce the possibility of breaking the rules and causing property damage by immediately being explicit about expectations and taking care of any problems before they become severe. This information is crucial when taking legal action, as it helps track down tenants who owe money or have caused significant damage. If tenants refuse to provide this information, it's a red flag indicating potential problems. However, specific issues remained despite these attempts, underscoring the difficulty of managing homes with renters who didn't always follow the rules.

These experiences highlighted the ongoing challenge of maintaining properties while enforcing rules. Whether related to property damage or late payments, each situation required careful attention to balance property upkeep and rule enforcement.

It wasn't just about fixing broken things or cleaning up messes. I ensured tenants followed my rules, like no pets or unauthorized modifications. This also included dealing with tenants who would change property features without approval, such as painting walls dark blue or brown, despite clear guidelines against it. This also meant addressing problems as soon as they came up and sometimes taking legal action if needed. Each situation required a careful approach to protect my property and ensure the rules were followed, making the job challenging and often stressful.

Based on my experiences, here is some advice on managing tenant relationships assertively while protecting your investments.

Start with clear and consistent communication. Be clear about your expectations from your tenants right away. This involves laying down in detail the terms of the rental agreement, the property's regulations, and who is in charge of upkeep. Confirm that the renters know all the guidelines and the consequences of breaking them.

From the beginning, clarify what is suitable and what is not. By clearly stating these rules from the start, you help tenants understand what is probable of them and reduce the chances of difficulties later on.

For example, highlight the significance of making rent payments on time and the possible consequences (such as late fines or the possibility of legal action) if they don't. In addition to preventing misunderstandings, open communication establishes the foundation of a civil landlord-tenant relationship. Make sure they can always reach you via phone or email about any issue.

If tenants break the rules, address the issues quickly. If you let it go once, they're more likely to do these things repeatedly. This might involve having a direct conversation or, if necessary, going to court to enforce the lease terms. Taking these steps helps protect your property and your investment. It's important to ensure that tenants follow the rules to avoid further issues and maintain the quality of your property.

While it's important to be firm when imposing rules, it's just as important to be fair. This means listening to what tenants say and taking their worries seriously. Sometimes, tenants may have particular problems or difficult circumstances that could make them act a certain way, but you must stick to the lease rules even then.

If a tenant shares an emotional story or tries to appeal to your sympathy to avoid paying rent, it's essential to remain calm and empathetic and remind them of the agreements they signed. For instance, tenants might plead for extra time to pay rent due to personal hardships, but I had to remain firm on the lease terms. You can manage the situation without letting emotions affect your choices by staying focused on the rules.

When it comes to handling repairs and complaints, approach these tasks systematically. Document all issues thoroughly and take the right steps to address them. For example, when a tenant damaged a ceiling fan or spilled Kool-Aid on the carpet, I meticulously documented the damage and initiated the repair process promptly. This organized approach helps track what needs fixing and ensures that repairs are done correctly. Maintaining a professional attitude and handling issues efficiently ensures that your property remains in good condition and that tenant concerns are managed fairly.

Maintain a professional distance from tenants. Being friendly and approachable is essential, but you should avoid getting involved in their issues. Don't let their emotional stories or problems affect your decisions. For example, when tenants tried to engage me in personal conversations or share their struggles to gain leniency, I kept interactions focused on business matters. Keep your interactions focused on the business side of managing properties. Ensure that rent and deposits are collected on time and follow the payment rules. Don't let tenants' financial troubles become your issue. If tenants fall behind on rent or cause damage, be prepared to take legal action to recover what you're owed.

Being a landlord means running a business, not offering personal help or support like a charity might. Your main job is to take care of your assets and pay rent on time. It's significant to remember that you are not there to provide financial aid or to get involved in tenants' problems.

You should always keep the property in good condition and ensure tenants follow their rent rules. This involves ensuring they pay rent on time and take care of the property. By staying professional and keeping a clear distance between business and personal matters, you can efficiently protect your investment and succeed in building healthy tenant relations. After 35 years as a landlord and a GM worker, I retired in 2020. My final experience as a landlord was particularly harrowing. At my last property on Court and Drive, tenants painted the living room dark brown despite my explicit instructions to keep it white. They also left a dog tied to a chair, who scratched the wall. When I confronted them, they didn't listen and continued to cause damage. I had to involve the sheriff to evict them, which was the last straw for me.

I realized that managing these properties was taking a significant emotional toll on me. Despite my efforts to maintain control and protect my investment, the continuous cycle of dealing with unresponsive and disrespectful tenants led me to give up being a landlord. I cried many times, feeling overwhelmed by the constant issues and feeling like nothing I could do was making a difference.

Since retiring, I've been trying to find my next purpose. I contacted Robert, who encouraged me to write a book about my experiences. Although I'm still figuring out what to do next, I strongly desire to sing and play the piano and guitar. I spend my days reading the Bible, praying for my team and the nation, and caring for my two kittens. Despite feeling lost, I remain hopeful. I have joy in my life since I left the landlord business and GM.

Since moving to Marion in 2004, I've observed a noticeable decrease in social contact within the neighborhood. The emergence of social media and the COVID-19 pandemic, which forced people to stay indoors for two years, have contributed to increased self-centeredness and disconnection. It is now more challenging to establish ties and preserve a sense of community due to growing isolation and a lack of neighborly assistance.

In conclusion, being a landlord requires a balance of firmness and fairness, meticulous documentation, and proactive measures to protect your investment. Despite the emotional and financial challenges, maintaining professionalism and clear communication can help manage tenant relationships effectively.

Chapter 15: Reflections on a Landlord's Journey

Good and negative memories flood my mind as I reflect on my thirty-five years as a landlord. Every year had its struggles and victories, but some lessons were more memorable than others. My path has been adorned with a patchwork of encounters that have influenced how I handle properties and perceive interpersonal interactions.

I was excited and full of hope in the beginning. I put much effort and money into my homes to make them feel comfortable for my tenants. I recall the several hours devoted to mending holes in the walls, servicing equipment, and ensuring everything was orderly. I knew a fair proportion of my renters had financial difficulties, so I equipped many of my apartments with refrigerators and stoves. Many worked at low-paying jobs and relied on government aid such as HUD to make ends meet. I wanted to provide them with more than a roof over their heads; I did want to help.

I made an effort but frequently felt like I was going in circles. No matter how hard I tried, I could never make them happy. Some tenants were grateful for my improvements, while others used my goodwill. I can still clearly recall my disappointment when several renters moved out, taking the appliances I bought to improve their living space. It was difficult not to take it personally because it seemed like a betrayal.

Despite my modest rental rates, it was depressing that many tenants refused to pay their rent on time. I kept my pricing modest, hoping it would benefit them, but I frequently thought my goodwill was misunderstood. This fact made it evident that, even with the greatest intentions, I did not influence how others viewed or appreciated my work. I would go above and beyond to meet their demands, but occasionally, this resulted in dissatisfaction when I didn't get the gratitude I had hoped for.

This taught me a crucial lesson: compassion does not always result in kindness being returned. Even though I put everything into my work, there were moments when it seemed one-sided. This was not always the ideal course of action for me, I would ask myself. My current self has been shaped by my lengthy and twisting journey, which included many periods of reflection.

Reflecting on what I've learned, I realize that I have gained knowledge about all aspects of human connection in addition to my duties as a landlord. I discovered that even though I could be helpful and encouraging, I also had to guard against being taken advantage of. While I thought providing my tenants with a nice place to live would inevitably result in positive relationships, this was not always the case. Many of them showed little regard for the place.

Setting limits and appreciating my values are now important, even though I still think assisting others is essential. This era of my life was ultimately about more than only possessions; it was about realizing how to find my position in the balance between giving and receiving. Despite all the obstacles I had to overcome, I came out on the other side wiser than before. I was able to use the things I've learned throughout these years to help me as I go on to the next stage of my life.

We didn't decide to start the next phase lightly. It happened after overcoming innumerable difficulties with renters and the requirements of property management. I tried to renovate and repair houses for years, ensuring my tenants had all they needed. I frequently went above and beyond by adding stoves and refrigerators to apartments to make them cozy places to live. When they first came in, many residents had very little; many were on housing assistance programs and frequently struggled to make ends meet despite working minimum-wage jobs. Creating a comfortable living environment might encourage a joyful and nurturing community.

But, despite my best efforts, I frequently received disappointment instead of the thanks I had hoped for. It felt like many of my tenants took advantage of my goodwill. After spending time and money on upkeep, I would find that some renters would vacate the properties without paying their rent or, in the worst-case scenario, would even take appliances with them. This was a hard lesson to learn: despite my best efforts to foster a happy atmosphere, some people didn't seem to care about the apartment they occupied or our agreements. I often felt that my efforts and good intentions were being ignored and that I was fighting an uphill struggle. Dealing with dishonest tenants took a significant emotional toll on me. Whenever a tenant neglected to make payments or abandoned the home, I felt I had failed personally. Feelings of betrayal added to the anger; despite my best efforts to be accommodating, my tenants frequently failed to provide the respect and accountability I expected. I used to get caught up in a vicious loop of hopelessness and disappointment, thinking things would improve just to have them fall apart again.

This never-ending loop of anxiety harmed my health. I had restless nights worrying about how I would shoulder the costs incurred by late rent payments, repairs, and maintenance. My relationships and health were both impacted by my growing anxiety. The delights of my profession were replaced by a feeling of burnout and disillusionment as my enthusiasm for building homes became a burden.

I noticed that I was withdrawing more and more as I felt the pressure of my obligations mounting. When my friends inquired about how things were going, I would try to be strong while breaking down on the inside.

For me, the circumstances reached a breaking point by 2020. After installing a brand-new carpet, I returned to one of my houses to discover that the previous tenant's dog had damaged the trim around the borders and they painted the walls dark brown. That was the final straw. I concluded that this industry was not suited for my kind nature. The unreliability of the tenant and the duties of being a landlord made it evident that this was not the right path for me. It was a sore awakening, but I had to put my contentment first.

It became imperious for me to leave property management to uphold my mental and emotional comfort. I began to reconsider my goals in life as well as my priorities. I no longer wanted to worry about neglected houses and unpaid rent. I started selling my homes and trading them for a loss to free myself of the weight that was beginning to get to me.

My fiancé was a great support system throughout this time, guiding me through the mounting costs of home maintenance and property taxes. He knew its emotional toll on me and urged me to find a solution. I stopped investing in homes that weren't making money since the financial strain got to be too severe. Being a landlord's business partner seems more like a trap than a source of fulfillment.

Reflecting on my path, I've discovered that self-care is as vital as resiliency. I concluded that putting my health before trying to win people over was necessary. I realized that if I wasn't taking care of myself first, I couldn't help others. I can't stress the value of being rigorous with tenants and ensuring they follow the lease agreement terms as guidance for those still in the real estate business. Checking someone's employment and background is important before letting them inside your property. The days of ignorantly trusting tenants are long gone.

Ultimately, through my experience, I realized that not everyone is cut out to be a landlord. It was a difficult lesson, and I decided to go in a new direction. My decision to leave the chaos behind has comforted me because the experience has shaped who I am. It was not an easy move, and sometimes, I questioned my decision, wondering if I would miss the relationships I had developed with my tenants. But those worries were greatly overshadowed by the tranquility I experienced in letting go.

I'm letting go of the disappointment and worry that came with my experience as a landlord and instead focusing on what makes me happy as I enter this new chapter of my life. I'm getting a new perspective on who I am outside of the landlord's duties.

I want to go into what I've learned about self-care, resilience, and the value of moving on after encountering hardship in the real estate business as I reflect on my experience as a landlord. In my thirty-five years as a property manager, I have faced many obstacles that have tried my patience. Every challenging tenant and every tense circumstance forced me to figure out how to adjust and persevere. Resilience is more than just getting back up after a hindrance; it's about taking what you've learned from it and applying it to advance.

I found my power and ability to overcome problems in the face of hardship. But I also discovered that a person's health and well-being shouldn't be sacrificed in the name of resilience. I learned so much about self-care as a result of my experiences. I frequently put my tenants' demands ahead of my own while working nonstop to resolve problems, maintain my homes in top shape, and foster positive connections with my tenants. I didn't realize how important it was to put myself first until I took a step back and reevaluated my goals.

As time passes, I realize how important it is to establish limits. My mental health is more important to me than merely keeping my possessions safe, so I'm rigid about adhering to lease terms. I discovered that standing up for my rights and saying no is OK. It is likely to avoid confusion and promote a more polite relationship with tenants by establishing clear guidelines and keeping lines of communication open. I started to see that being firm and fair with my tenants did not imply that I was horrible; it meant putting my health and the truthfulness of my properties first.

Life will inevitably involve adversity, and the real estate sector is no different. But instead of seeing it as a roadblock, I now see it as a chance for improvement. Every obstacle I overcame gave me priceless insights about accountability, trust, and the significance of doing my research. I urge everyone starting in the real estate industry or going through a difficult time to view these impediments as opportunities rather than barriers. They can be worthwhile educational possibilities that set you up for success in the future.

Accepting that I couldn't alter other people was one of the hardest things I had to do. I expected that by showing kindness and encouragement, I would encourage my tenants to do the same. However, the truth was that I was only in charge of my reactions and actions. Thanks to this knowledge, I could release the resentment and irritation holding me down. I learned to see each event as a reflection of their circumstances rather than a reflection of my value as a landlord and to stop taking their behavior personally.

I'm concentrating on the things that make me happy and fulfilled as I begin this fresh phase of my life. I can pursue new interests and pastimes, spend time with family and friends, and live a healthy lifestyle. Leaving the pressures of property management behind has allowed me to take advantage of fresh opportunities I would not have known about.

I feel great and thankful as I conclude this chapter of my life. In retrospect, I see that every challenge I overcame, and every tenant I encountered significantly influenced the person I am today. Despite the difficulties I faced as a landlord, I also learned a lot of lessons that I will never forget.

I'm happy I participated in the race. I was young when I started, full of ambition and hope. However, thanks to my tenants, I've matured into a wise, experienced woman. I've learned more from you than I ever could have dreamed. You showed me the reality of the rental business, the complexities of human behavior, and the significance of setting limits while offering compassion. I admit that my journey to becoming a landlord was neither easy nor flawless. There were moments of hurt, rage, and frustration.

I wouldn't trade those years for anything else, though, despite everything. Thanks to them, I've grown and understood who I am and what matters in life. I appreciate every tenant who came into my life because they taught me the importance of self-care and resilience.

I stand here now as a landlord and someone who has overcome adversity and found more inner peace. I now understand that life is about finding balance and knowing when it's time to let go and go on rather than just doing business and taking care of properties.

I want to thank every tenant who shared with me during my trip. You have been essential in my progress and self-discovery. You helped me realize the highs and lows of being a landlord and, more significantly, how crucial it is to pursue personal fulfillment in addition to my career.

I'm ending this chapter with a lighter heart and a more composed head. I can't wait to welcome the next phase of my life, which promises more possibilities, fresh starts, and optimism. Even though I'm leaving the property management industry, I'm taking the priceless knowledge you've given me.

Let us toast to new beginnings, acquired knowledge, and a fantastic path ahead.